Finding Bertie

Susan M Arrowsmith

© Susan M Arrowsmith 2015

All rights reserved

No part of this publication may be reproduced, distributed, or transmitted in any form or by any means, without the prior written permission of the author, except in the case of brief quotations embodied in critical reviews and certain other non-commercial uses permitted by copyright law. For permission requests, contact the author.

ISBN-13: 978-1511989343

ISBN-10: 1511989343

Design & formatting by Socciones Editoria Digitale

www.kindle-publishing-service.co.uk

FOR DEREK
WHO MADE THE JOURNEY WITH ME

FOREWORD

I was born in 1943 during the Second World War. At the time of my birth my mother, Rose, was married to her second husband John Musker. There was a mystery surrounding my birth that was never explained to me. My mother was fond of recounting how my 'father' had caused a scene at the hospital where I was born and had to be escorted from the ward. But why should this be? My early recollections of him were of a caring and kind man. When I was six years of age my parents divorced and I did not see John again for over thirty years.

When I eventually did trace John, who I still believed to be my father, it was through a radio request programme but it was a troubled reunion. Despite this we continued to meet regularly over the next few years. Towards the end of his life John confessed to me that I was not his daughter and that my mother had had an affair with a soldier whilst he was away. The name of my real father was Bertie 'Chalky' White.

This is the amazing true story of my search for my biological father and how, with only the flimsiest of evidence, I retraced Bertie's tragic footsteps and found, at last, my way home.

PART ONE
'CHALKY' WHITE

CHAPTER ONE

Looking back over my life it amuses me to remember how different I was from the others. Like a summer cuckoo in a nest of town sparrows. I can see us all still living in that ground floor flat at 111, Lancefield Street in Paddington, Mum, Mary and me and my little brother John. This was during those years after the Second World War, when our road, like most of London, was littered with bombed out buildings and in some places huge craters in the ground marking the spot where once houses and small factories had stood. Here, we the local children, loved to play in defiance of our parents, careless of the dangers of collapsing walls and unstable floor boards.

There were three families sharing the old Victorian House that we called home. The Meelings, a large, noisy family of Irish immigrants, who occupied the top floor. Whilst the Smiths, a quiet middle aged couple, were sandwiched between us, the Muskers and the Meelings. We were the lucky ones who occupied the ground floor and so had use of a tiny, overgrown back yard. In my memory no attempt had ever been made to cultivate it. It was mainly used as a dumping ground for such items as the tin bath we used in front of the fire on bath nights and Mum's mangle, together with John's outgrown pushchair. Yet, as far back as I can remember it was a special place to me.

Even then, as a small child, I was fascinated by growing things and by the wild birds that came looking for bread in our backyard.

They were sparrows mostly but occasionally a blackbird or a thrush flew in from nearby Queens Park. The birds were my friends and I gave them all names and laid out my dolls tea set in the garden with cups of water and plates of bread for them to feed on. Flowers never grew in our yard but all sorts of hardier weeds struggled for survival. I dreamed of a real garden, like some of those I passed on my way to school, where I could make flowers grow. On day, in a fit of indulgence, my elder sister Mary dug up a small patch of earth and here I tended my weeds, or, 'wildflowers' as Mary tactfully called them.

What did Mum think as she watched me growing up? Did she ever think about my father? If so she gave no hint to his identity that I can recall. But then she had many other problems to occupy her mind.

Mum was a war widow. Even after her third marriage she still liked to call herself so. She had married Mary's father Albert, who was a regular solider, in 1935, four years before the outbreak of the Second World War. Sadly, he was killed in Belgium in the early part of the war leaving Mum a widow, before her twenty first birthday, with a small daughter to bring up. She didn't stay single for long and two years after the death of her first husband, in 1942, she married Dad. It was one of those hasty war time, whirlwind courtships and marriages that was doomed to fail. I was born in 1943 and my brother John in 1946, after the war had ended. Their marriage was over before my 6th birthday and Dad soon disappeared from our lives.

Somewhere in the back of my mind I have vague memories of a kind, jolly man who carried me around on his shoulders. Someone I called 'daddy', and who I watched for each day, on the wall outside our house, to come home. Until one day he did not come home at all. It would be over 30 years before we met again.

Life must have been extremely hard for Mum when she found herself once again a single mother with three children to bring up. This was before the welfare state as we know it today and for those without means of support there was only the National Assistance Board. Mother was forced to apply for assistance because dad was in prison because he refused to pay maintenance for us children.

She had to face the humiliation of having the man from the Assistance Board come and look round our spartan home for anything she could sell before she was awarded a piddling amount of money which barely covered our food and rent.

One particularly awful Christmas when Mum simply did not have enough money to buy each of us a single present she was in despair. But we were in for a great surprise. Even in those dark days there were a few philanthropic people around ready to help the needy. One of these was a lady called Mrs Edith Soames, a rich widow who lived in the West End of London. Mum never found out how she came to knock on our door just days before that particularly hard up Christmas. Mrs Soames was like a fairy godmother to us and not only brought us all presents but loads of food and decoration to put up. She became a good friend to Mum but sadly died from cancer in 1951. She also took a fancy to me and Mum told me much later that she had asked if she could adopt me as she thought I was a bright and pretty child. I have often thought of how different my life would have been if she had adopted me and I would have been Susan Soames and mixed with all the best in society. But that was not to be.

During the intervening years, as part of the post-war slum clearance, we were moved to a council house in Dagenham. To my joy we had a real garden with two apple trees, one that regularly produced a crop of cooking apples and the other eating apples. For my birthday I was given a child's set of garden tools and some real vegetable and flower seeds. Blissfully happy I cultivated my own little patch of earth and to everyone's amazement I grew flowers and vegetables in abundance. From somewhere I had this innate knowledge of how to make things grow; a need within me that found expression in my garden.

Dagenham, with its neat privet hedges and little gardens seem a rural paradise compared to war torn London but it was on a school holiday to Epping Forest that I first discovered the delights of woods and trees and fields, of baby rabbits and wild primroses. Here I was first aware of a feeling of oneness with the countryside which I had never experienced before. As I grew up this yearning to be close to nature remained with me and I realised that I had a connection with the earth that was central to my very being. When, at the end of my school holiday, I returned to Dagenham I sensed that I was in the wrong place. Nowadays, my husband Derek and I live amidst the gentle countryside of South Norfolk and my spirit is at peace.

Mum married for the third time in 1959 to a man she had been friendly with for some years. When Pender moved in with us it was a difficult time of adjustment for us all. Mary, John and I felt ourselves to be displaced in Mum's life. Firstly by her new husband and then by a demanding baby, our sister Elisabeth, who was born two years later. At the time it seemed that our house was full of tension and constant rows with things becoming increasingly intolerable at home. Now, I can sympathise with my mother, who was suffering with post-natal depression, but in those days this condition was not taken seriously by many GP's and there was little treatment available.

Sundays, when we were all together at home, was the worst of times. I was 18 years of age and engaged to Derek and we had planned to marry in the coming September, which was still seven months away. So, it was not surprising that on one particularly awful Sunday morning, when Mum had worked herself up into a rage over some minor misdemeanour on my part, that she screamed at me that she 'wanted me out of her house and I could pack my suitcases and go'. I was not wanted. This was by no means the first time she had made similar threats. but I had had enough and I did not want to stay in a house with a 'mad' woman and a screaming baby. So, I calmly packed my suitcase and then went to the phone box and called a taxi, and asked the driver to take me to Derek's parents' home.

Derek's mum and dad must have been astonished to see me climbing out of the taxi but they hid their feelings well and opened the door to me. Derek was still having his Sunday morning lay in and was rudely awaken by his mother banging on his bedroom door to break the news that his fiancé was waiting for him downstairs. Thankfully they did not suggest I return home to my mother but as their house only had two bedrooms, and this was an age when unmarried couples did not openly sleep together, they had to find somewhere for me to live until we were married.

In the end I stayed with Derek's aunt Rosie for several months before I returned to my family home. But I did not return until the date of our marriage had been brought forward. Derek and I decided there was no point in my going back to a family situation where my mother was finding it increasingly difficult to cope with three grown up children and a baby. If I left home Mum would have one less person taking up space in what was by then an already overcrowded house.

Derek and I went to see the vicar for the second time and explained the situation to him. He was extremely kind and understanding and said the earliest we could be married was the 26th May at 4 o'clock in the afternoon. I gladly settled on this day and time and Derek and I went away to notify our friends and relatives. I learned later that Mum had been spreading a rumour that I was pregnant but I can honestly say that was not so. Our first child David was not born until two years later. However, the 26th May has an important significance to this story as we were later to discover. What made us decide on that particular date? Was if purely chance?

Like most young couples the early years of our marriage were taken up with establishing a home and raising a family. Our son David was born in 1964 followed four years later by our daughter Samantha in 1969. When I became pregnant with David we put our name down on the council housing list in the hope of renting a council house as our parents had before us. Up until then we had privately rented some rooms in the house of an elderly couple but our lease had a clause that stated 'no children', so we were forced to leave and move in with Derek's parents when I became pregnant. We submitted our housing application to the local council and were dismayed to be told we would probably have to wait six years before we reached the top of the housing list. I knew that several of the young married girls I worked with had obtained mortgages and so were able to buy a property on the private market. Derek and I decided to take this option but soon found that any privately owned properties in Dagenham or Barking were way out of our price range. We had no alternative but to move further away. In the end we settled for a house in Frindsbury in Kent within an hour's commuting distance of Derek's job in London. One bonus for me was that for the first time in my life I was within walking distance of the orchards and green fields of Kent.

CHAPTER TWO

In all those years since Dad left home when I was six years of age I had never heard a word from him. Often, around Christmas and my birthday, I would think about him. What was he doing? Had he remarried and had other children? Did he ever think about me? Could he really be as awful as Mum portrayed him? Was he even still alive? These were the thoughts that dominated my mind as I approached my 40th birthday. I reckoned that by now he must be reaching retirement age. I realised that if I wanted to see my father again time was running out. My search must begin soon but if I were to begin my search where should I start?

Even after so many years, asking Mum for help was out of the question. Her hatred of Dad was still evident whenever she talked about the past. When we were children she had to struggle on her own, without a penny paid in maintenance, a fact she was fond of reminding us. Therefore, the search for my father had to be a secret. I dare not even take Mary or John into my confidence in case they told Mum. I pondered long on where to begin. Dad's address at the time of the divorce was in Liverpool but that was over 30 years ago and I would have to ask Mum for that. Then my daughter Samantha gave me an idea. She told me about a friend's mother who had written to a radio request programme for help when trying to trace a long lost uncle. The programme was on radio 2 and broadcast every Sunday afternoon, it was called the 'Charlie Chester show'.

In the end it was all so easy. One of the advantages of Mum's new marriage was that she was known by her new name and lived in a different area where it was unlikely she would be identified by Dad's surname. Apart from that I knew Mum wasn't in the habit of listening to the radio, especially radio 2. Before I had time to change my mind I typed out my request to Charlie Chester and walked to the post box and mailed my letter.

The next six weeks were nail biting tense and we listened in religiously every Sunday to the programme. The Charlie Chester show was aimed at the older generation and played music of the era favoured by this age group interspersed with requests from listeners. It was on the sixth Sunday that we finally heard Charlie ask for news of one John Musker, last heard of in Liverpool and London, for his daughter, Mrs Susan Arrowsmith from Kent, who has not heard from her Dad in over 30 years and would very much like to do so. The message could not have taken more than a couple of minutes, yet as I listened I was aware of what I can only describe as a feeling of warmth reaching out to me. In that moment, without a shadow of doubt, I knew my message had been heard.

A week passed and I began to think I had been mistaken. I waited daily for a letter, for the phone to ring. Nothing! Then, half way through the following week, quiet early in the morning I happened to be upstairs in our bedroom. I heard a car pull up outside our house and glancing out of the window I saw it was a taxi parked by our front gate. A small, tubby, elderly man, in overcoat and hat was, with some difficulty, climbing out of the car. For an instant my heart seemed to stop beating and I knew, even before he knocked on the door, that the daddy I had waited so long to come home, was here at last.

CHAPTER THREE

There were no hugs and kisses as might be expected on such an occasion. We just stood there, stupidly gaping at each other. He was the first to speak.

"Do you know who I am Susie?"

I hadn't been called Susie in years.

"Yes.......you're my dad."

The floor seemed suddenly to reach up as I felt myself about to fall.

"Here luv," he was over the threshold taking my arm to steady me, "sorry if it's a bit of a shock, me turning up like this."

"I thought you would write or telephone....or something."

"Was going to luv...but in the end it seemed better to just come."

We had moved into the living room by this time and we both sat down,

"I could do with a drink," I said, "we might have a drop of sherry in the larder".

"Good idea luv...you look a bit shook up and I could do with one myself."

I went shakily out to the kitchen and raked around the bottles in the bottom of the larder. "Good! just about enough for a couple of glasses," I called.

As I poured the sherry I began to realize I wasn't properly dressed I was wearing only a night dress and a dressing gown. As I was a nurse, after a spell on night duty this wasn't unusual at this time of day but god knows what Dad thought.

"I'll have to get dressed," I said handing him the sherry, "I've been working nights. I'm a nurse you know. I was just about to get dressed when I saw the taxi."

"A nurse," he sounded pleased, "might have guessed you'd turn out to be a nurse, you loved dressing up in your nurses set when you were little."

It struck me as strange that someone who was a complete stranger should have such intimate knowledge of my early life.

I raced upstairs to get dressed and as I did so I realized I was terribly excited, just like at Christmas when I was a little girl. A little voice in my head was saying "daddy has come home....daddy has come home," just as if I were a small child.

An hour later, when Derek came home from the shops, Dad and I were seated together on the settee shifting though all my old photos.

"This is my dad," I said lamely, "this is Derek...he's my husband and has just been to the shops."

"Though he must be."

They shook hands formally.

"We were beginning to think you hadn't heard the message, "said Derek.

"Oh I heard it all right" he said thoughtfully, "strange that was. I'm not usually at home on Sundays, I go to see friends but they were away on holiday, so I just happened to turn the radio on when I got back from the pub. I couldn't believe it when I heard my name...after all those years...my little Susie."

"Did it give you a shock.?" I asked.

"More than a shock I can tell you," he smiled, " I gave them on the programme a ring right away and the girl at the other end said they would write giving me your address and telephone number". He paused for a moment reflecting, "I waited all week and then got onto them again, Seems they were moving to another studio but I got your address out of them in the end." He sounded pleased with himself.

"What did you do then?"

"Looked you up on the map......thought Strood was in Gloucestershire?"

"No that's Stroud."

"In the end I asked a mate on the station and he put me right, so I got the train from Charring Cross this morning. When I got off at Stood the taxi man knew where your road was."

He beamed at me quite clearly delighted with himself. "Better than winning the pools when I heard your message. Yes, it was better than winning the pools."

I laughed, "you haven't told me anything about yourself. Where do you live? Did you meet any one else after the divorce?"

"No", he looked sad, "there was a lady in Liverpool but that was a long time ago now. We lived together for a while but I was a bit too fond of the drink. It didn't work out, so, I moved back to London. Lived in Whitechapel for 20 years now. Worked for Unilever most of that time, in the stores. Until they made me retire last July," he replied unhappily.

In fact Dad had lived in a men's hostel in Whitechapel for all those years. It seemed incredible to me that he had never really tried to make a new life for himself after the split with Mum. I remember Mum telling me, when she was in one of her more mellow moods, that Dad had been orphaned when he was 5 years old. He was brought up in a catholic orphanage by monks. Perhaps this was another factor in the break-up of their relationship, Dad simply had no role model for how an ordinary husband and father is expected to behave.

Later that afternoon Derek drove him back to Strood station as he was eager to be home before the London rush hour. He promised to come again for the day on the following Sunday which was a bank holiday weekend. I kissed him on the cheek and I could see that this pleased him. Strangely enough it was quite a natural gesture on my part. Somehow the years between seemed to have rolled away. I was grown up but he was still my daddy.

He came again the following Sunday and we drove down to Whitstable for an afternoon by the sea. David and Samantha came with us because they were curious to see this long lost grandfather. Dad came armed with sweets and treats and soon won them over. He had an easy personality and a lively Scouse sense of humor, yet at times I could sense he was not as much at ease as he tried hard to appear to be.

In those early days of our new relationship I felt curiously at odds with myself. On the one hand I was ecstatic that I had my father back in my life. I had always been aware of the gap he had left. Now that void was filled. Yet, I was increasingly aware of a feeling of resentment growing within me. Resentment for all the years of childhood neglect. For all those Christmases and birthdays he had ignored. I recalled how he went to prison rather than pay my mother maintenance. He told me so himself, as if he was proud of the fact. A blow of defiance at my mother without thinking about my brother, without thinking about me. These thoughts festered away at me, eating me up, spoiling our relationship. I was open with him about the way I felt. Sometimes, when I was at work sitting up at night with my private patient I would write him long letters. Some I posted, other I destroyed. He was kind and understanding, did not try to excuse himself. He was willing to accept our relationship on any terms. On my terms. But I didn't know what I wanted.

Years later, when I went to seek counseling for another reason, I talked about this time in my life with my counselor. She told me these conflicting emotions are common with adopted children. On one side the abandoned child longs for a relationship with its real parent; on the other the critical adult asks why? Why? Why?

The months went by and these conflicting emotions grew stronger. One day I would write to ask him to come down, then I would write again and cancel the visit. We planned a trip to his home town of Liverpool to visit some of his relations that he had not seen in years. At the last moment I phoned to tell him I could not go. In the end he went alone.

Inevitably the mental pressure became unbearable. This was a dark period of my life as I struggled with increasing bouts of depression.

When I felt well enough I still wrote to my father, even visited him in London. Dad was suffering from Parkinson's disease and as the years went by he found it increasingly difficult to travel. Once, after visiting us at home, he fell down the steps at Strood station. From then on I went to see him in London. He still lived at the hostel so we got into the habit of meeting for lunch in his favorite pub in Whitechapel High Street.

Some years after that first meeting I received a curious letter from him saying he would like me to come and see him again as he had some 'family business' he wanted to discuss. Dutifully, I wrote back and arranged to meet him in the usual place a week later.

He met me at the station that day. He was waiting for me at the top of the stairs as I came up from Whitechapel underground station. As always he was delighted to see me but he seemed nervous, tongue tied, which was unusual for him, as we walked the short distance to the pub. His hand shook violently as he tried to pick up his drink.

"Must have had a drop too much last night," he said jokingly.

"Is it the Parkinson's," I said more seriously.

"Maybe...I've not been too good lately."

"What does the doctor say?"

"Not a lot...gave me more pills."

I ate my salad and Dad ate a roll. He didn't like eating in public because he was afraid of spilling his food. Then, over another drink, I broached the subject of my visit. Again he appeared nervous. I had the feeling he was already regretting sending that letter.

"Is it something to do with your health," I suggested at last.

"In a way, though it's nothing serious. But one of the reasons I wanted to see you was because I've been to see a solicitor and made a will."

"Oh! I see."

"Not that I'm thinking of popping off yet," she said jokingly. There's life in the old dog yet...but I wanted to get things settled...do what's right."

"You don't have to worry about me Dad."

"I know that luv...it's not that I've got much to leave. Just a bit left out of my pension money. But I'd like to have a decent funeral, they cost a bit and what's left over is for you".

"Then spend it Dad," I said. "I'd much rather you spent it now than save it for me."

"No, I want you to have it. To make up a bit for what you didn't have as a kid". He covered my hand with his shaky one. "You know I love you Susie....you were my little baby....my little pride and joy." His voice broke with the emotion and I squeezed his hand.

"I know Dad. I know it wasn't all your fault. Mum is a difficult woman, even I left home in the end."

He smiled "She was a right one your mother always had a terrible temper. And that reminds me I have got something for you."

He rummaged in a carrier bag he had brought with him. "I've been sorting out at home and found some old photos that I thought you might like."

I laughed as we went through the pile of faded, old, black and white photos. There was one of me taken when I was about three in Trafalgar Square. Typically, I was kneeling down feeding the pigeons from a bag of seed.

"Oh look! All those curls. I never have been able to manage my hair," I laughed. Then looking in the bag and finding one of my mother. "I remember this one...you used to carry it around in your wallet. I remember you showing it to me when I was a little girl."

The photo must have been taken in a studio when my mother was in her mid-twenties. She was smiling and beautiful almost serene in a way I had never seen her. At some time the photo had obviously been torn in half and was now stuck together on a card.

"Your mother gave it to me when we were first married. Years later she tore it up after we had one of our rows."

"Typical, I can see her doing that."

We fell into conversation about the past. He told me how he and Mum had met in the Swan pub in Hanworth where she lived with her parents through part of the war. Dad was on leave from the army after the retreat from Dunkirk They met and married before Dad was shipped back overseas to fight in the war once again.

"Were you away long?"

"A couple of years. Then I got sent home, I was invalided out of the army in 1943 My chest you know," he patted his chest.

"I see, so when you left the army you and Mum got back together again?"

He paused for a moment considering his reply then said," your mum didn't want to come back to me. He fell silent then continued. "You see she met someone else while I was away and they had an affair."

"No! That was rotten."

"Yes, he was a paratrooper. Sergeant Chalky White they called him."

"Chalky is an odd name," I remarked.

"All those who are named White are called Chalky in the forces luv," he explained, "Chalky, white, get it," he laughed before adding, "his real name was Bertie White, or so I believe." He then became more serious and I could tell that he was drifting back into a long, lost past. "Chalky White and your mother wanted to get married," he continued. "They came to see me when I was in hospital....him and her...he said he wanted me to divorce her so that they could get married. He wanted to do the decent thing."

"What did you say?"

"Told them no way...it's against my religion...I'm a catholic you know."

"Yes, I know and I'm one too. So what happened?"

"Nothing!" he seemed to shrink into his chair, they went away together but in the end she came back. Yes she came back and then you were born."

He looked at me earnestly as if weighing his next words then continued, "You were born in Paddington hospital."

I remembered what Mum had told me about my birth.

"Mum said you were drunk and made a scene when you visited her in hospital after I was born," I said accusingly.

He looked at me sheepishly and replies, 'yes, I had had too much to drink and said things that I didn't mean. Next day I felt very sorry about it and went to the hospital intending to make it all might with your mother.

"What did she say?"

"She said she was sorry too and she offered to get you adopted. Said we could make a fresh start. Have a child of our own."

Something like a bolt of electricity seemed to pass through my head.

"She wanted to get me adopted!" I looked at his face and then I understood. "Oh god! I see. So you are not my father?"

Dad was shaking now and his eyes had a haunted look as he looked pleadingly into mine.

"I told her not to even think about it. As far as I was concerned you were my little girl, my little Susie and that was how it was. I went to the registrar office and I registered you myself on that same day. With my name."

The mystery that surrounded my birth has been explained.

"You are not my real father," I repeated slowly.....I see it all now. That was the reason why you had that argument with Mum in the hospital. I am not your daughter?" I was crying now. "So who is my father?"

Dad was crying now and he did not answer my question.

"Was Chalky White the paratrooper my father?" I said at last.

He nodded at the same time patted my hand but his emotion was so great he was unable to speak. We said no more on the subject on that day or ever again. Afterwards, many, many times afterwards I regretted not asking him more. But at the moment I knew how hard it had been for him to tell me. He had said enough. He chose to tell me the truth knowing he might lose the only person he loved. And truth to tell, perhaps, at that point in my life, I did not want to know. Finding one father had caused me enormous emotional distress. I was not ready to put myself on the firing line again. Not just yet.

I traveled home on the train in what I can only describe as a state of shock. With a few words Dad had effectively turned my conception of myself upside down, It was true that Dad and I had spent many years apart, that he had little influence on my upbringing, but I knew enough about his background to give me a sense of identity. Now even that was lost.

Derek and I had spent the best part of a year before my reunion with Dad researching the Musker family tree. The family originated in Liverpool and as part of my research, I had spent several days in Liverpool searching through the old parish records for mention of my ancestors. Now all my lovingly documented family charts were meaningless, a waste of time. And in its place I had only a name, Sergeant Bertie (Chalky) White, nothing more.

Thinking back it seemed unbelievable that I had lived all those years with Mum without even a hint. Yet, maybe I had missed something I began to search my memory for traces of a clue. The difference in my character from those of Mum, Mary and John had always been obvious. My love of growing things and animals was only the tip of the iceberg. I was like chalk to cheese as far as they were concerned. And then there was my relationship with Mum. In a way that had always been difference. Apart from that time when Mum was suffering from post-natal depression we had rarely quarreled. True I had often been caught up in her rows with Mary and John but her anger was seldom aimed solely at me. But why? Did she sense something different in me that would not take such arguments lightly? Something that reminded her of my paratrooper father. If so, she had been right, look at the way I packed my suitcase and left that day her anger was aimed at me.

Other memories came flooding back. Mum had always referred to Dad as 'old Musker' never as 'your father' to me. Yet, when she was angry with John she often screamed at him 'you're just like you ****** father'. And what about the way I looked? The carriage was empty so I stood up and surveyed myself in the mirror above the seat. There was a familiarity to Mum, we had the same colour eyes, but what about the shape of my face, my stubborn chin and curly hair? These were not like my mothers. Were they inherited from my paratrooper father?

With those thoughts upper most in my mind I made my way home to break the news to Derek. I was amazed when he told me he wasn't at all surprised it had been something he had suspected all along.

"I was more surprised that day when you told me he was your father," he confessed.

"But why?" I asked.

"Because you're nothing like him, you don't look like him, you don't act like him."

"Maybe that's because I hardly know him."

"No, it's more fundamental than that. You have drive and ambition, but look at your Dad, he's a nice enough bloke but put yourself in his position, can you see yourself living in a hostel for over 20 years?"

No, I said reflecting, "I could never understand why he has never tried to find a place of his own. When he was working he certainly earned enough."

"And what about all these plants and animals, he gestured round the room, "we are surrounded by them. We can't move for them in this house."

I laughed, "I wonder what Chalky White was like?"

"I bet if we could see him right now he'd probably be out tending his garden, or allotment, with a couple of old dogs at his heels, like those two there."

I glanced down at my two Yorkshire terriers sitting under my chair, "I think he'd go for something a bit bigger." It was a pleasing picture but as I thought about Chalky White I felt a coldness, a darkness inside and my intuition told me that he was dead.

It was some months before I saw Dad again and nothing had changed between us. In fact, if anything our relationship improved because I could begin to understand why he had never tried to find me. He probably thought I knew he wasn't my father. His health gradually deteriorated to such a degree that Social Services deemed him a suitable case for sheltered housing. They moved him into a new complex of flats for the elderly with warden supervision. For the first time in his life he had a key to his own front door. A home of his own. I went to see him a few days before Derek and I moved to Norfolk. He was frailer now but appeared more cheerful than I had ever seen him.

Dad was able to enjoy his new home for almost two years until his condition deteriorated still further and he was moved to a nursing home at Herne Bay. Why he chose to spend his last remaining days at Herne Bay, far from his friends in the East End? I can only guess. Maybe he had pleasant memories of our Sunday together when we all went out for a day at the sea and stopped off at Herne Bay to walk along the beach.

I was at work when the telephone call came. It was Derek to tell me that Dad was very ill, not expected to last the night. Rushing home I hurriedly packed a few things into a suitcase as I anticipated we would have to stay the night.

We arrived at the nursing home at around 8pm. The day staff were going home and the matron had waited to see us before she left. Thankfully he was still alive but she had given him an injection of morphine for the pain and he was not really conscious. They had moved him to a small room on his own. There was just enough room for a bed and a chair and the furniture was shabby and old. The room seemed cheerless, devoid of personal possessions, with a single light in the center of the ceiling, lighting the room and the floor was bare but for some brown linoleum. Yet the night staff seemed kind and caring.

At first I did not recognize him, he looked shrunken and unnaturally pale, his eyes were opened but I could not tell if he knew it was me. I spoke his name and his eyelids fluttered in some form of comprehension. I sat on the bed holding his hand and gently talking to him, telling about the children; remembering the past. The hours passed slowly and gradually his breathing changed and I realized he was slipping away. In the early hours of the morning the care assistants came to turn him. They suggested we go and lay down in the room matron had prepared for us. We were both very tired but I do not think either of us really slept. I lay there, taut and listening, haunted by memories of the past, of all that might have been.

At around 7am we were awoken by a care assistant. Dad had just died peacefully in his sleep.

When the care staff had washed and changed his body, ready for the undertaker, I went to see him for the last time. Now that the pain was over he looked tranquil like a sleeping child. I knelt and said a prayer to our Lady that his soul might find peace, as I felt this was what he would have wished.

We carried out his instructions for his funeral to the letter. I informed his relations in Liverpool but they did not come, they sent flowers in their place. In the end there was just Derek and me and two of the care assistants from the nursing home to hear his catholic burial mass. Yet, the service was carried out with dignity and I do not think he would have asked for more. I had ordered a wreath of two dozen red roses to place on the top of the pine coffin. He was so light the pallbearers carried his coffin with ease. After the service at the church Derek and I drove out to the crematorium overlooking Canterbury where, after a short address by the priest, we committed his body to the flames.

My heart was heavy as we made the long journey back to Norfolk. Dad and I could not have met more than a couple of dozen times since that first meeting. But I knew that he had loved me unconditionally, accepting me on my own terms. And in my way I had loved him in return. I felt my life would be the poorer by the loss of his love.

Some time later I received a letter from the matron of the nursing home containing a building society deposit book in Dad's name. It contained just over £4,000, which he had saved for me out of his small private pension, starting from the month we first met.

CHAPTER FOUR

There were times after Dad disclosed that he was not my real father when I was tempted to tackle my mother about her relationship with Chalky White. I felt I had a right to know. Yet, my mother had kept her secret for so long now how could I tell her I knew the truth about my birth? How could I ask her about my real father without telling her about my meetings with Dad? So the months, the years went by and the right moment never came.

Since my marriage Mum and I had never been very close. It was almost as if once I left home she has washed her hands of me. Moving to Norfolk meant our meetings became fewer and fewer. That is not to say I was not always there when she needed me. She knew she only had to phone, or, get my younger sister Elisabeth to phone and I would be there.

So, when in the summer of 1993 I had a telephone call from my younger sister Lis to tell me Mum was ill and had been taken into hospital and would I like to visit? A few days later Derek and I drove to Basildon Hospital to visit her. I had not seen Mum for a some time so I was taken by surprise by her appearance when I saw her in the hospital bed. She had lost a great deal of weight and looked so frail I was afraid of hurting her when I sat on the edge of her bed. Even at 74 she was still an attractive woman. Her hair was pure silver and still thick, she wore it longer than she used to which suited her. Her skin was remarkably fine and almost free from wrinkles but it was the magnificent high cheek bones that gave her face that striking appearance.

She seemed genuinely pleased to see me and wanted to know all our news. Our daughter Samantha had married the previous summer and was now expecting her first baby. We looked at the photos I had brought to show her. Samantha always had been her favorite. When I told her she would soon be a great-grandmother she looked wistful and said she hoped she would live long enough to see the new baby. Sam had been ill throughout her pregnancy with morning sickness. I remember how sick Mum had been when she was pregnant with Lis and I reminded her on the fact

"I was always sick when I was pregnant, but it didn't see to do any of you any harm, you were all strong, healthy babies," she remarked proudly.

From then her thoughts seemed to go back to the past and she began to retell how I was born in St Mary's hospital, in Paddington during the war. A story I had heard many times but this time I listened with more interest. Would she give me a clue to the identity of my father?

"You were a breach birth, I had two doctor's trying to turn you."

"That must have been awful," I said sympathetically.

"Yes, I was very poorly," she said quietly. Then her mood seemed to changed, "and that old sod Musker turned up as drunk as a lord and the nurses had to throw him out."

She went on to tell me once again the story of how Dad had subsequently spent all her savings during the time she was in hospital with me. As a child I somehow thought this was my fault. It was my father after all who had treated her so badly. Now I knew all the facts. If only I could find a way to maneuver the conversation in another direction.

"Yes I know he treated badly, " I paused not knowing what to say, " but he's dead now," I finished lamely.

"Oh!" she looked at me seemingly uncomprehending.

I waited to see how she was taking this news "I met Dad several times before he died," I said more boldly, "I wanted to see for myself what sort of man he was."

Still she looked at me blankly and I remember that Lis had said Mum was often confused nowadays. I sighed, what was the use in upsetting her now. I turned the conversation to safer ground, asking about her illness, and she told me about what the doctors had said and how the nurses were treating her. She gave no clue as to what she was really thinking.

A week later she was back home with Mary and it was soon after this I received a letter from her. The letter began clearly enough thanking me for visiting her in hospital and saying how glad she was about Sam and the baby. Then the tone of the letter changed dramatically and her writing became muddled as if written in great haste, but she stated clearly 'that old bastard Musker was never your father. You don't have a drop of his blood in your veins. My God, she understood. Then, maddeningly the letter went on about how badly she had been treated. Not another word about who my father was. "But it is a start," I said out loud , " and next time I see her I'll tackle her, I'll get the truth once and for all."

Fate was against me once again and a few days later Lis telephoned to say Mum had been taken ill and was now back in hospital after suffering a stroke. Once again Derek and I made the mercy dash to Basildon. This time she was in a little side ward on her own. The nurse in charge came out to speak to us in the patients waiting room before I was allowed in to see her. She wasn't too bad but the stoke had affected her speech, for the moment at least, she wasn't able to say a word. I went in alone to see her. She was attached to a drip because they said she had become dehydrated. I sat with her for some time but she grew restless and I could tell my presence upset her. So, I left her, hoping that in time she would recover.

Weeks went by and gradually Mum did improve but she seemed too confused, unable to understand what had happened or where she was. The medical staff said she might recover and plans were made to find her a place in a nursing home. I went to see her again but on this occasion she seemed completely unaware of who I was. I did not go again.

December came and Mum was moved into a local nursing home in time for her 75th birthday on the 13th December. Shortly after that she caught a chest infection and her condition rapidly deteriorated. By Christmas the doctor told us to be prepared for the worse. All over the Christmas holiday we waited for the phone to ring. But the old year drew to its close and still mother hung tentatively to life. She died on the morning of the 2nd January 1994.

It is a terrible moment when one learns a parent has died no matter how difficult that relationship might have been. Somehow now all the old family quarrels seemed so futile, such a squandering of precious time. Yet, I was comforted by the thought that I had always tried to make our relationship work.

My young sister Lis had the unenviable job of making all the funeral arrangements. Living so far away there was little for me to do but wait. My thoughts were now once more in the past and the unanswered question of the identity of my father. It seems strange to say but in some way I felt a unexpected sense of relief. As if, while Chalky White identify remained a mystery , nothing was expected of me. More to the point I would expect nothing of myself Whereas, if my mother had revealed his identity, and how I could trace him ,it was in my character to follow any lead come what may. Now I would have to be content to let Mum's secret die with her.

A week passed. Life went on much as normal. My present job was working in a residential home as a nurse on call on Tuesday and Thursday nights. The job required me to be in attendance if any of the residents were taken ill during the night. Most nights I retired to bed at around 11pm, leaving the care staff on duty to call me if necessary. So it was that on that Tuesday night, two days before Mum's funeral, that I retired to bed in the little room allocated to the nurse on call. I remember being particularly tired that night, having spent the morning shopping in Norwich. All was quite in the home and I looked forward to a good night. I set my alarm clock for 6am and soon fell into a deep sleep.

At some time during that night I had a dream. In the dream I was alone and in some dark place. As if I were in a thick fog and could not see my way ahead clearly. Suddenly, I was aware of stumbling, and then being caught up in something clinging, and sharp so that I was unable to move, like a butterfly in caught in a bramble. Each time I tried to move the thorns pierced deeper into my flesh.. I realized that the more I struggled the more entangled I became, so, in the end, I lay there in the dark, waiting, waiting for something or someone to free me.

Then I heard a voice that I recognized as that of my mother. At first I thought she was calling my name, "Susie", but then I realized what she was actually saying was just one word, "Bertie". I listened attentively, trying to work out what the direction the sound was coming from. Then she called again, more urgently, 'Bertie', there was no mistaking the name as she repeated it again and again, "Bertie, Bertie, Bertie."

I had a feeling that she wanted to be sure that I had heard her so I said the name out loud , "Bertie."

There was a pause for a while before she spoke again and this time she said, "17th September", and then once more, "17th September."

"17th September," I repeated dutifully. Then waited to see if she had anything else to say?

Then the tone of her voice changed and with a terrible sadness she cried "Arnhem, Arnhem, Arnhem, Arnhem," over and over again as if her heart would break.

"Arnhem," I repeated softly, ..."Arnhem."

After that there was silence and just as suddenly I was free of whatever it was that had held me and I was no longer afraid.

I did not wake after my dream but instead I must have fallen into a deeper, dreamless sleep because I remember nothing more until I was awoken by my alarm clock the following morning. It was time for me to get up and help the girls give the residents their breakfast. There was no time to ponder on the meaning of the dream but every detail was still clear and fresh in my mind. I have always had a strong belief in the power of dreams and I believe that certain dreams have an important significance for the dreamer. Not those every day dreams, that we all have, when our subconscious mind regurgitates every day events from our waking lives into a dream; or the wish fulfillment dreams when we are living out our fantasies; or even the nightmares when our deeper fears surface, tied up in terrifying metaphors that represent those fears. The significant dreams I am talking about are different. Throughout my life there have been occasions when I have dreamed about certain person, or, a particular place and a short time later I have found myself in just the situation I dreamed about. There is a story in our family of how, when I was a little girl, I woke screaming in the night saying granddad had fallen off a ladder and hurt his leg. Sure enough a few days later this exactly what happened when granddad went up on the roof to replace some loose tiles and lost his footing and ended up in hospital with a broken leg. Those who knew my grandmother say I have inherited her 'gift', her psychic abilities and I am sure this is true.

It has always been said in my mother's family that my grandmother Ellen had the sixth sense and was well known in the village where she lived as a 'seer', that is someone who is able to foretell the future. She read the Tarot for anyone who asked her and often had significant dreams similar to those I have experienced. They say she had a dream the night her son-in-law was killed in action in the Second World War in which he told her he would not be able to come home and asked her to take care of his wife and their little girl. Two days later the telegram boy brought the telegram from the War Ministry saying Albert had been killed in action when fighting the Germans in Belgium. There are countless stories about granny Ellen and I could fill a book with tales of her psychic encounters, but this is my story so back to my dream at the nursing home.

The hours until I left the nursing home that morning seemed to drag and I put my mind to getting my tasks finished so that I could leave on time. As it happened I was delayed because when I was giving out the morning medicines I found that one of the elderly ladies was unwell with a high temperature so I sat with her until the day nurse came on duty. It was around 9am when driving home I could go over all the details of the dream. It was all so vivid, being lost in the fog and trapped by some invisible force but mostly my mother's voice repeating the name 'Bertie' and the date '17th September', and the anguish in her voice as she repeated 'Arnhem, Arnhem, Arnhem,' over then again and again. Had this been a significant dream? It is said that the recently dead often visit loved ones in their dreams during the period shortly after their death. Had my mother come back in spirit to tell me what she had failed to tell me in her lifetime? The identity of my father, or was I being fanciful. Should I put the whole thing down to the fact that my mother's funeral was due to take place tomorrow? Yet, the name Arnhem, rung a bell in my head. I felt sure it was a famous battle but if of the First or Second World War I could not recall. Then there was the date the 17th September what possible significance could that be?

When I finally arrived home Derek had already left for work and the house was empty. He worked for a firm of insurance brokers in Norwich and kept to normal 9 to 5 office hours. I work at the nursing home covering the night shift on two nights and on these days we are like ships that pass in the night. When I come home after a night shift I have the house to myself so I usually have a shower followed by a leisurely breakfast but today I made straight for my study which houses my collection of books. Somewhere I had a ' Chambers book of Dates', this is a reference book, similar to a diary, with a section for each day of a year. Each date contains a collection of historical facts of events and other interesting information, such as the birth or death of some famous person that had occurred on that day in a particular year.

It took me just a few minutes to find the book that I was looking for and I placed it on the desk in front of me. I realized that I was shaking as I skimmed through the pages looking for the entry I wanted. "Yes, here it is," I said triumphantly, "now let's just see."

I thumbed through the pages until I reach 17th September, turning over the page I read 1944 ' On the 17th September until 26th, 1944, The British airborne invasion of Arnhem and Eindhoven in the Netherlands took place - the operation was called 'Operation Market Garden.' British and American and Polish paratroopers were dropped behind enemy lines in the Netherlands to secure key bridges and towns. On 17th and 18th September a large airborne force of around 1500 aircraft dropped the British and American paratroopers near their target. Unfortunately heavy German army resistance pounded the allied forces until they were forced to retreat. Nearly 1500 British paratroopers died in the attempt and more than 6500 were taken prisoner. Although at the time Operation Market Garden was regarded as a failure , future generations have viewed the battle as a benchmark of stoicism and determination.

And so it was true. The Battle of Arnhem did take place on the 17th September in 1944. I read and reread the entry several times trying to make sense of it all. Dad had told me that my real father was a paratrooper and if that was truth then there was a strong possibility that he had fought in the battle of Arnhem. Maybe he had been one of the many who had been killed in action? One thing that was certain was that I would do everything in my power to uncover the truth.

CHAPTER FIVE

I sat for long while just staring at the entry in the 'Chamber's Book of Dates', trying to make sense of it; looking for a rational explanation. But there was none. Even if it were remotely possible that deep down in my subconscious there was a connection between the battle of Arnhem and the Paratroop Regiment there was no possible way I could have known the exact date, the 17th September. It just did not make sense. This led me to an even bigger question, the date of the battle of Arnhem was correct and so was the name of my real father, Sergeant Bertie White. So, was my dream a message from my dead mother who, at this very moment, lay in her coffin awaiting her funeral?

I thought about granny Ellen who had a strong psychic sense and often predicted things that would happen in the future that seemingly she had no way of knowing. I remembered she often told us about her dreams and how, on rare occasions, someone who had died, or as she would have said 'passed over into spirit', would return in her dreams with some message or prediction for the future.

There had been many occasions in the past when I had been aware of my own strong psychic s sense. I often know when someone is about to telephone me even before the phone rings. Derek and I have a telepathic link and sometimes there is no need for me to ask him to bring something from the shops, he will already be on his way home with it. Then there was the terrible day when Derek's mother died suddenly and unexpectedly of a heart attack. The last time I saw her was a week earlier at her golden wedding anniversary when seemingly she had been fit and healthy and on her best form. I was in Scotland, at an Open University summer school course for a week, when she died. The first two days I was at summer school where great. I was at Stirling University and loved mixing with other students who were doing the same course. Then, on the Monday morning and I was inexplicably by feelings of fear and sorrow that seemed to come from nowhere. I phoned Derek to make sure everything was o.k. at home and he said they were all fine but I knew inside that something was badly wrong. As I put the phone down I had a flash of intuition, my mother in law had died. It didn't make sense but I knew that she was dead.

I could have rung back and asked if it was true but something held me back. Derek didn't want to tell me so I kept the knowledge to myself. Later, Derek told me he didn't tell me because he felt certain his mother would have wanted me to complete the Open University course. When he met me at Victoria coach station the following Friday he broke the news to me.

"I've got something awful to tell you," he began to say, as we sat in the car.

I beat him to it. Before he had time to finish the sentence, I said. "You're going to tell me your mother died last Monday?"

"How did you know....did someone else ring and tell you?"

"No, I had one of those strange experiences I get from time to time. It was last Monday morning, when we were all in a lecture, when out of the blue I had this terrible feeling as if something awful had just happened but I didn't understand where the feeling was coming from. Up until that moment I had been enjoying the course. Loving every minute. Do you remember when you telephoned that evening?" I paused . "It was as I put the phone down. It just popped into my head that your mother had died. But it was not just a thought it was an absolute certainty as if you had told me yourself."

"She died that very morning," he told me sadly, "it was completely unexpected. Evidently she thought she had indigestion and she came downstairs and sat in her special chair. It was there she had a heart attack and she died before the ambulance could get to her."

***

I was still pondering over these thoughts when Derek arrived home for lunch. He instantly knew something was wrong.

"You won't believe this, in fact I really can't believe it myself, but I think I know where and when my father died," I said.

"I can believe anything as far as you are concerned," he replied soberly, "now tell me all about it."

I went through my dream again, telling every detail, leaving nothing out. Having to put it into words made it sound too far fetched. Impossible.

What do you make of it?" He said thoughtfully when I had finished.

"I just don't know. I've tried to find a logical explanation but there isn't one. The date and the battle of Arnhem meant nothing to me before this morning. It doesn't make sense," I paused to collect my thought. "But in a way it does make sense and that's what's so frightening about it."

Derek looked thoughtful, "it does add up, if 'Chalky' White was in the Paratroop Regiment as your Dad said then it is possible that he was killed at the battle of Arnhem."

"Do you know anything about the battle of Arnhem?"

"Yes, I read loads of war books when I was a kid and I've always had an interest in the World Wars. The battle of Arnhem is the most famous Airborne Invasion of the Second World War". He thought for a few moments and then continued, "If I remember rightly it was a plan thought up by Montgomery to capture key bridges over the Rhine to allow the advancing allied army to cross into Germany. The Brits drew the short straw and were told to take the bridge at Arnhem. Trouble was these just happened to be a SS Panzer Division of Germans waiting for them, particularly on the second day, the British paras didn't stand much of a chance but they put up a good fight."

"You seem to know a lot about it," I said impressed.

"Yes, I've read about it and there was that film, 'A Bridge too Far'", he replied.

"So, there is a strong possibility that Bertie, alias Chalky White, died at Arnhem?"

"Very many did. The whole thing went badly wrong from the start."

"And if Bertie died in 1944 that ties in with my birth in 1943."

"He would have been around in 1942 when you were conceived."

I considered this information then asked, "how are we going to find out if a Sergeant Bertie White of the Paratroop Regiment was killed at Arnhem?"

"There must be army records."

"Yes, of course, but where are they and how am I going to get access to them?"

"You could try asking at the reference department in Norwich Library, at least they should be able to tell you how to go about finding army records."

"Yes, I could start there but it will have to wait until after Mum's funeral tomorrow."

With that sobering thought I turned my thoughts to preparing for the sad journey the following day.

The day of the funeral was cold but bright with a weak January sun lighting the sky. We were both quiet on the car journey from Norfolk to the Essex crematorium. We had arranged to meet the funeral cortège and Mum's friends and relations in the funeral chapel at the crematorium and we arrived in good time. A service was already in progress so we sat in a gloomy waiting room, There was a list of the day's funerals on a notice boards and I saw my mother's name. Rose Buckley. I had seen it written many times, now with a jolt the reality of the situation hit me. A feeling of nausea swept over me. I got up quickly and walked outside to get some air. At almost the same moment the funeral car appeared and I stood silently watching as the undertakers carried my mother's coffin into the chapel. 'Where was her spirit now?, I mused, 'was she here with us?' As the undertakers carried my mother's coffin into the chapel, I promised silently, 'I will find out what happened to Bertie.' Almost immediately the feeling of nausea lifted and I felt a sense of inner peace.

***

Saturday arrived and Derek and I made the promised trip to the Norwich reference library. A helpful librarian at the reference desk looked through the records on possible genealogical sources and said that the Army records for the Second World War were unavailable at present to the general public. She did tell us, however, that the Register of Births, Marriages and Death at St. Catherine's House, London, held details of all Forces deaths recorded during the war years and these were open to the public. We had found our first positive line of investigation. As St Catherine's House was only open on weekdays we would have to wait until we could both take a day off work. In the meantime I had to content myself with browsing round the shelves of the general lending library for booked about the battle of Arnhem.

I began by reading General Robert Urquart's book, 'A Bridge Too Far', on which the film of the same name is based. General Urquart led the 1st Airborne Division, the famous Red Berets, in the attack on the bridge at Arnhem. The order from Montgomery was to hold the bridge for two days, they held if for nine days, before they were forced to retreat.

The first wave of the Airborne Army left England on Sunday 17th September, followed by a second wave on the 18th September. Things went badly wrong from the start. Urquart was cut off and driven into hiding for the first hours of the battle. The 2nd Parachute Battalion captured the key Arnhem road bridge on the first days suffering severe casualties in the process. There was fierce fighting for 9 days and those who had taken the bridge were cut off from the other battalions. There were many casualties among the Airborne troops, some were forced to surrender to the Germans, others managed to escape. It was one of the worse defeats of the war.

As my knowledge about the Paratroop Regiment and the battle of Arnhem grew, so, I began to build up a picture of the kind of man my father might have been. The Paratroop Regiment was still in its infancy in 1944 and the paras were all regular soldiers who had volunteered from other regiments. The training, as now, was very tough and only the fittest and most determined stayed the course. Those who did were issued with the famous red beret and became part of the Airborne Army. I guessed that my father must have had the courage and the determination necessary to make the grade.

I was fast becoming an expert on the battle of Arnhem. I read everything I could get my hands on. Derek often came home from work to find me head in a book.

"I never thought I would see you so interested in war books," he remarked one day.

"I never had cause to until now," I replied, "but I must say I feel a bit ashamed of being born during the war and knowing very little about the main battles."

"Perhaps our generation was too close to the war," replied Derek. "My relations were always going on about the war when I was a kid, especially at Christmas when they all got together. In the end you get so bored you just switch off."

"Mum was always talking about the bombing of London and the rationing but I can't remember much else," I said thoughtfully. "Although I do recall that she talked about Mary's father who was killed in France." Then an idea came into my mind, "one thing I do remember though is that he was buried in a war cemetery and her having a photograph of his grave. Do you think that Bertie White could be buried in a war cemetery at Arnhem?."

"Possibly," he said thoughtfully, "we will have to do a bit more research."

"Urquart mentioned, in his book, visiting a war cemetery at Oosterbeek. If I remember rightly he said that, after the war ended, every September the Dutch people have held a memorial service at Oosterbeek. Many of the veterans and the families of those who died go there year after year."

"Just by coincidence this year will be the 50th anniversary of D Day so it must also be the 50th year since the battle of Arnhem."

"We could go to Arnhem in September," I said excitedly, "we could try to find Bertie White's grave."

From then on the idea began to grow in my mind. Somehow we would go to Arnhem in September and find my father's grave.

I made a few enquiries and found a travel company, Holt's Battlefield Tours, who were arranging a tour to Arnhem in September to attend the commemorations. I rung the company and a girl at the other end said she would be pleased to send me a brochure and 'yes' it would be possible for me to visit the war cemetery at Oosterbeek. A few days later the brochure arrived and enclosed with this was a leaflet which was far more interesting.

"Look at this," I said to Derek, "it's a leaflet from the Commonwealth War Graves Commission telling how to trace a war grave."

"You could write to them."

"Better than that there's an application form on the other side." I said studying the form. "Seems all I have to do is fill in the details and send it to them."

"At least that will prove one way or other if Bertie is buried out there."

"Yes, there wouldn't be much point going all that way to Arnhem if they can't trace his grave, " I said reflectively." I think I will send this form off now and leave booking the tour until we are certain."

It didn't take me long to fill in the form; Name - Bertie White, Regiment - Paratroop Regiment; When and when died' Arnhem 17/25 September 1944. I sighed there wasn't much to go on. Would that be enough? All I could do was post the form and wait.

Weeks passed and I heard nothing. I pushed the Holt's Battlefield Tour guide to the back of the kitchen draw. If there wasn't a grave there was no point in going to Arnhem.

"I promise I will go to Arnhem if they find a record of his grave," I said out loud.

I found the envelope laying on door mat some days later. I could see the 'Commonwealth War Graves Commission', printed on the back of the envelope. I picked it up and fled upstairs where I could open it in private. With an unsteady hand I drew out the letter and read as follows:

Dear Mrs Arrowsmith

Thank you for your completed Location Enquiry Form. I can confirm the following information from our records;

Sergeant Bertie White, 6977506, serving with the 156th Battalion Parachute Regiments, Army Air Corps, died on 18/19 September 1944, age 32 and is buried in Plot 5, Row B, Grave 10 in Arnhem Oosterbeek War Cemetery, Netherlands. We also hold the additional information that he was the son of Abraham and Elizabeth White. Arnhem is situation at the confluence of the Rhine and Ijssel. Oosterbeek is a village 7 kilometers west of Arnhem on the north bank of the Rhine and on the road to Wageningen. The cemetery is to the north of the village. I hope the above information proves helpful.

Yours sincerely, (and signed),

Marie Choules, Enquiries Section.

So, it was true, my father, Sergeant Bertie White had been killed in action during the battle of Arnhem. The implications took my breath away. But there was one thing I was certain of, I intended to keep my promise and find his grave, with this intent in mind , that afternoon I posted my cheque to Holt's Battlefield Tours. When Derek came home from work that evening I was able to tell him that we would be going to Arnhem in September.

PART TWO

ARNHEM

CHAPTER SIX

Now that I had proof that my father, Bertie White, had been killed at Arnhem so my feeling began to change. The feelings of curiosity with which I had begun my search were replaced by an unexpected, often overwhelming, sense of sadness. Sadness for the brave young man who had been killed. Sadness for grandparents who had lost a son. Sadness for myself, the little child, who had missed so much because her daddy had been killed in the war.

My thoughts often turned to thinking about my grandparents who, in other circumstances, I might have known and loved. It was fifty years since Bertie died so logic told me they were long since dead. Gone to their graves never guessing that part of their son lived on in me. I brooded on the past, thinking back over the years to all the times my mother might have told me about my father the day I was married, or, when my son David was born. Surely, on these milestone days in my life, her thoughts must have turned to the man she once loved, Bertie White? There were so many things I wanted to ask her. What did my father look like? Where had they first met? Where did his family come from? So many questions left unanswered, so much left unsaid. But Mum was in her grave. Dead! She was beyond my reach.

For most of my life I have suffered with depression and at times it has been a struggle coping with the extreme mood swings this condition can bring. Now my moods swung irrationally as if I were on an emotional yo-yo. It just so happened that I was due for one of my twice yearly appointments to see Dr Kitson, a consultant psychiatrist, who has looked after me through my dark days in the past. I was initially referred to Dr Kitson after my brother John committed suicide and my depression spiralled out of control.

Fortunately for me with his help and modern medicine my life has improved dramatically. However, I was well aware of how emotional turmoil could throw me off balance. It was with some trepidation that I disclosed the purpose of my proposed trip to Arnhem.

"I realize that I could be stepping into an emotional minefield," I said to doctor Kitson after I had told him the story, "but I feel very strongly that I have to see this through, I have gone too far now to turn back."

He did not try to put me off but smiled at me across his desk, "I understand why you want to do this Susan and why you need to discover all you can about your father."

"It seems that half of my life has always been a lie," I replied quietly, "I have no family history on my father's side, half my background is a void."

"This is a journey you are ready to make." He paused for a moment and looked at me with concern, "I am not going to put you off doing so because you are emotionally stronger than when you first came to see me after the death of your brother but make no mistake it will not be easy.

"I realise that doctor."

"Then take care of yourself, he smiled again, "just monitor you emotions and if you feel yourself going too low then come and see me again."

We parted and I felt more cheerful than I had for some weeks. Dr Kitson had given me his blessing to make the journey to Arnhem.

***

It was early June and the media was full of stories about the events taking place in this country and in France to commemorate the D-day landings. I remember watching a service broadcast from one of the Second World War cemeteries in France. Along with the dignitaries and senior members of the armed forces were some of the original D-day veterans. They were old now, the youngest of them must have been at least 68 years of age, but they wore their medals with pride. Once the service was over the television news team followed them as they placed poppy crosses on the graves of comrades who had not been so lucky. I could see row after row of identical headstones and I realised this was how it would be in the cemetery in Oosterbeek. How would I feel when I was faced with the reality of my father's grave?

***

It was shortly after the D-day commemorations that I had a series of dreams that were to prove to be of significance in the future. The dreams were similar in that I was always standing on the edge of a pavement, at a cross roads, in a place I did not recognize, the strange thing was that, although this was obviously a main road, there was no sign of any traffic, not even a parked car. In one direction to my right the road climbed up a hill so that I could not see what lay beyond this point. As I waited at the curbside other people gradually came to join me, young and old alike, some with children in tow and even babies in prams and there was the gentle hum of their voices that grew as the number of sightseers increased. No one ever spoke to me but I was quite at ease, it was as though this place was somewhere I was familiar with and had been many times before. As the crowd gathered so a feeling of excited anticipation grew. We were waiting for something or someone; but for what or whom? Then faintly at first I thought I caught the sound of music and then the marching sound made by many pairs of feet coming from somewhere beyond the hill. I waited and strained my ears expecting the sounds to grow louder, and for those who marched to appear over the brow of the hill, but to my disappointment after a while the sound faded away and the crowd began to disperse.

Each time I had this dream the sequence of events was the same; waiting at the crossroads, the gradual appearance of the crowd, the feeling of excited anticipation. The only difference was that with each dream the sound became louder and appeared to be nearer. I could make out the sounds of drums and flutes and the marching feet. I was certain they would soon appear from over the hill. Yet no one came into sight and each time I was disappointed. On the last occasion they sounded so close that I was certain they would come over the brow of the hill at any moment. With a sudden flash of revelation I realised that my father was out there with them. That it was he who I was waiting to see. It was he I could hear marching and playing in the band. The sounds began to fade away and I was afraid I would lose him. I stepped out into the road and ran up the hill to try to catch up with them.

"Wait for me....wait for me....I'm coming....wait for me," I yelled into the darkness, the sound of my own voice woke me and I sat bolt upright listening, listening in the silence. All was quiet but I knew in that moment, that my father was waiting for me. He was anxious for my coming. He had waited for 50 years.

CHAPTER SEVEN

Derek and I were reading the newspapers over lunch, as we usually do, when Derek spotted an article in The Daily Telegraph he was reading.

"Look at this," he said, "some of the Arnhem veterans are planning a parachute jump to commemorate the 50th anniversary."

"They're brave, they must all be getting on a bit by now."

"It says here that the youngest is 68 but that's not the point, one of the veterans interviewed was in the 156 battalion of the Paratroop regiment at Arnhem."

"The same as my father," I said excitedly, "let me have a look."

Sure enough one of the three Arnhem veterans interviewed by the Telegraph defence correspondent was Les Lockett, 73, of Stoke-on-Trent, a former private in 156th Parachute Battalion.

"He might have known my father."

"Even if he doesn't he might know someone who did," replied Derek.

"How do I get in touch with him?"

"The article was written by The Telegraph's defence correspondent so why don't you write to him enclosing a letter to be forwarded to Mr. Lockett."

"Yes, I'll do that now before I forget."

Later that day I wrote a carefully worded letter to be forwarded to Mr. Lockett asking him if he remembered my father sergeant Bertie White, who was killed in action at Arnhem. I explained that

I had only recently learned that Bertie White was my father after my mother died. I was careful to avoid any mention of my dream. I didn't want Mr. Lockett thinking I was a head case. Not just yet.

Mr. Lockett did not take long to reply he wrote back giving me his telephone number and asking me to ring him which I did the same evening.

"Hello, Mr. Lockett, it was kind of you to write to me."

"Hello dear, nice to get your letter," he sounded kind and friendly. "Now I don't remember your dad myself, there were a lot of us, and we tended to keep to our own NCOs ," he paused, "but I'm the secretary of the 156th veterans association so I might be able to find someone who does. I'll have to ask around a bit, but have to be discreet."

"Thank you so much Les it will mean a lot to me to contact someone who actually remembers my father. I have no memories of him and now that Mum is dead there is no one to ask."

"She kept the secret all her life?" he sounded surprised.

"Yes, all her life," I said bitterly."

He must have caught the note of bitterness in my voice.

"Don't blame you Mum love, things were very different when we were young and it wasn't done to have a child out of wedlock."

"But it happened all the time during the war."

"Yes, but people still didn't like it."

"But to keep it a secret for 50 years," I said defensively, "my father was a war hero and she couldn't even tell me."

We talked for some time. It seemed that Les had been wounded when parachuting into Arnhem on the same day as my father. Fortunately for him he had been picked up by the Dutch and treated in hospital before being interned as a prisoner of war until the war ended in 1945.

"I was one of the lucky ones who came back but so many of my mates weren't as lucky" he told me sadly.

"It will be hard for you when you jump in September, reliving the memory of Arnhem."

It will be hard for us all love, those of us who survived, we never can forget Arnhem, it's always with us. But we go back every September as a mark of respect for our fallen comrades. Those like your Dad who never came home.

I realised the tragedy was still and always would be with him "I'll remember that when I see you jump in September." I replied.

We were silent for a moment as we shared our grief and I was aware of what Arnhem meant to those like Les who had lost so many of their comrades. The loyalty they felt to those who had died.

Les and I kept in touch but sadly, we was unable to trace any of his comrades who remembered Sergeant Bertie White. Then, a few weeks before we were due to leave for Arnhem, Les did have some news for me.

"It's not much I'm afraid love but we have been over to Oosterbeek training for September so I took the opportunity of getting some information for you from the Dutch records.

"That was kind of you Les, what is it?"

"The least I could do love. What I did find out is that your Dad died sometime between the afternoon of the 18th September and the morning of the 19th. The Dutch picked his body up on the DZ, or dropping zone to you."

"Oh! I see," I paused taking in this information, "would that have been on Ginkel Heath?"

"That right, same place they picked me up."

"So, he could have been killed whilst actually parachuting into Arnhem?"

"Very likely," I could hear the emotion in his voice, "they were waiting for us with bloody machine guns, just picked us off. We didn't stand a chance."

"It must have been terrible?" I said sympathetically.

"Yes," he sighed, "a nightmare, you know I still have nightmares, after all this time."

"I'm sorry Les," my words sounded inadequate even to my own ears. What could I ever really know. But he did not seem to notice.

"It was probably all over very quickly for your dad," he said kindly. The Dutch took care of him and saw to it that he was buried decently."

"And after the war they moved him to the Oosterbeek war cemetery," I asked.

"Yes, along with his mates. Gave them all full military honours," he said proudly, "and ever since then we have gone back. Just to let them know they are not forgotten. Just so they know we remember."

I could feel the tears running down my cheeks as we said goodbye. I wept then, for my father Bertie White and all who died with him and also for those like Les who have spent the rest of their lives remembering the tragedy of Arnhem.

CHAPTER EIGHT

Only weeks to go before we set out for Arnhem with Holt's Battlefield Tours, but there was one thing left to do. That was to arrange a day to go to London in order to search the public records of Births, Marriages and Deaths at St. Catherine's House and obtain a copy of my father's death certificate.

It was a sunny, Monday, morning when Derek and I took the train from Diss to London, arriving at Liverpool Street station at around 11am.

"It shouldn't take long to find my father's death certificate," I said confidently, "we know exactly when and where he died."

"If we get finished early perhaps we can go on to the war museum," said Derek, "I believe they have a special D Day exhibition and there might even be something about Arnhem."

"Might as well make the most of our day in London," I agreed.

Once at St Catherine's House we asked direction to the Army War Records of deaths during the Second World War and were directed to a small section containing the relevant records. As I had anticipated, it didn't take long to find the entry for Sergeant Bertie White. I filled in the request form and paid the fee to the girl behind the counter.

"We won't be able to collect it today," I explained to Derek, "they send them through the post the lady said it usually takes about a week."

It had taken us less than half an hour to find the entry.

"It seems a pity to have come so far for one certificate, "I said thoughtfully. "Why don't we search the records of births for a copy of Bertie's birth certificate. My father was aged 30 when he died on 18th September 1944, that means all we have to do is look at the birth records between 18th September 1913 and September 1914, it shouldn't take long."

We found the section containing the births ledgers. As expected there were very many entries under White. An hour passed and we had looked through all the entries for White during the relevant year but found nothing for 'Bertie White' with parents Abraham and Elizabeth.

"What now?" said Derek, "Do you think we have missed it?"

"I don't think so," I said puzzled, "I checked every entry. Now let me think." An idea came to me and I said, "maybe his age on the death certificate was incorrect. Let's take it a year either way. You take 1912 and I'll try 1915."

Time passed. It was 1 o'clock and still no sign of the elusive Bertie White. My eyes were beginning to feel the strain and I was hungry. We worked our way to the end of the files for years 1912 and 1915 without a trace and I felt at a loss as what to do next.

"Let's take a break for lunch and think it over," suggested Derek.

I had packed a picnic lunch so we made our way out into the sunlit London street. My eyes were momentarily dazzled by the brilliant light.

"Let's walk down to the Embankment and find somewhere to sit," I suggested, "there are some gardens near the Embankment underground station."

We joined the tourists and office workers who were taking their lunch break in the sunshine. It was pleasantly warm and we relaxed in the shade under the tree providing a sanctuary from the busy London world. Strange to think I lived in Paddington, just a short bus ride from where we were now, for the first six years of my life. It seemed worlds away from our quiet Norfolk home.

"Do you want to go back to the records office and search some more?" asked Derek breaking into my thoughts, or, shall we call it a day and go on to the War Museum?"

"We may as well go back to the records office and try again," I replied, "we won't get the chance to come again before we leave from Arnhem."

Reluctantly we packed away our lunch things and returned to St Catherine's house to resume our search. The records office was quiet now, most of the morning people had disappeared.

"Let's each try another year," I said, "you take 1916 and I'll take 1911."

Thumbing through the entries I was beginning to feel a sense of failure. I reached the end of 1911 without a trace of what I was looking for. I could see Derek was nearing the end of 1916.

"Nothing," he said closing the final volume, "it seems that Bertie White never existed.

"Perhaps we missed it," I replied despondently.

"Shall we go through then again?" Derek asked patiently.

And so we went back to the beginning and checked them all once again.

"It's almost closing time," said Derek at last, "we're going to have to pack up and go home."

"O.k. just let me finish this last volume." I skimmed through the final entries before having to admit defeat.

The attendants were tidying up and so, with the few remaining searchers, we were forced to leave. Most of our day spent in the public records office had proved to be a complete waste of time.

"I just can't understand it," I said on the train home, "Bertie's birth must have been registered. It's the law. So how could we have missed it?"

"Perhaps he was born overseas," suggested Derek.

"We will just have to wait for the death certificate to find out," I said wearily, "that will give us his place of birth."

Once again I waited for the postman each day. Then, exactly a week later my self addressed envelope came through the letter box.

Derek watched as I tore it open. I took out the black edged death certificate. It was scant in information. Nothing that we didn't know already. Except!

"You won't believe this," I said with a laugh, "no wonder we couldn't find an entry for my father's birth."

"What then?" Derek said eagerly.

"It seems, my father, Bertie White, was born in Northern Ireland."

"So Bertie was probably Irish?"

"Yes, that is why his birth wasn't registered at St Catherine's House, it is most likely he was registered in Dublin."

"White doesn't sound like an Irish name," said Derek, "perhaps his parents were English and just living in Ireland at the time of his birth."

"Not everyone who is Irish is called Murphy or Kelly," I replied laughing, "but I have this feeling that Bertie White was Irish through and through."

"But there is something else you have overlooked!" He paused for effect, "if Bertie was Irish then you are also half Irish."

"Now that is a strange thought." I mused, "but one thing is certain. No more Irish jokes in this house."

CHAPTER NINE

September came bringing the first touch of autumn. We were to leave for Arnhem on Friday 16th September. Holts' tours had arranged for us to travel by coach from Victoria coach station to Dover and from there by P & O Ferry to Calais. From then on the journey would be by coach to the hotel Mercure in Nijmegan. Rather than make the journey from Norfolk to London on the Friday we decided to spend Thursday night with our daughter Samantha and her husband Andy, who lived in Kent, thereby reducing the journey time to London, and the risk of arriving late. It would also give us the opportunity of seeing our baby granddaughter Chloe.

Chloe, at that time, was 18 months old. She was a pretty, intelligent, happy child who also suffers from cerebral palsy. Chloe has been disabled since birth, when during a very difficult labour, she was starved of oxygen and consequently suffered brain damage. For the first few days her life hung in the balance. Then, seemingly she made a good recovery. But by the time she was six months old it was obvious to her parents that their baby daughter was not progressing at the expected rate. At 8 months the consultant diagnosed, what they already suspected, Chloe had cerebral palsy. Exactly how much this will affect Chloe's life is uncertain but that she will be disabled is certain.

It was some months since I had last seen Chloe and, as always, my pleasure at the prospect of seeing her was mingled with a feeling of unease for her future. Under normal circumstance Chloe had reached the age when she would have been able to toddle out to meet us. Instead, we arrived to find her sitting in her specially designed high chair. She looked bright and happy but I could not help thinking about the prospect of Chloe spending her life in a wheelchair.

The following morning, September 16th, dawned wet with a strong wind blowing. It would be a rough Channel crossing. Derek and I were up and ready to leave before the family were out of bed. As the taxi arrived to take us to the station, I realised it was today that I was to begin my pilgrimage to Arnhem and I felt a cold, hard feeling in the pit of my stomach. At the station the early morning commuters were crowding onto the trains. To them this was just another working day. To me it was to be a journey of self discovery, a journey to find my roots.

The train pulled into Victoria just before nine. We made our way to the coach station where we were we to meet the Holts' representative and our fellow travellers. Our luggage bore the official orange ' Holts' labels and we pinned the orange name badges to our coats. It didn't take us long to locate a group of people similarly adorned. This being the 50th anniversary of the battle of Arnhem, there were to be 6 coaches with around 280 people in all traveling to Arnhem.

Once assembled in our groups we were introduced to our party leaders. Our leader was Colonel Nic Grey, an ex-army officer, who was accompanied by his wife Anne. Colonel Nic had recently retired from the Army and told us that he was now supplementing his pension by acting as a tour guide for Holts'. The colonel was all hale and hearty with lots of military banter. It was Anne, the colonels lady, who was the organizer, he would have been lost without her. Most of our fellow travellers were middle aged or elderly men and a few had their long suffering wives in tow. Many were Holts' tour veterans who made a habit of regularly visiting the sites of great military battles.

We reached Dover in time for the 12.30 ferry. As I had anticipated a strong wind was blowing and the channel crossing was choppy. For a time at least fear of the ferry sinking outweighed any others thoughts. When we eventually docked in Calais it was time to get back on the coach for the long, tedious journey through France and Belgium to Holland. It was early evening when I caught sight of the first road signs to Arnhem and

Nijmegen. Up until then these places were only names I had read about. In my mind they were associated with the death and destruction of war. Today, they are pleasant, leafy modern towns like many others in Europe. It was hard to make the connection with the images of the past with the reality of the present.

At long last, the coach drew up outside the hotel Mercure. We were all travel weary, wanting nothing so much as a good meal and a clean bed. Dinner was served at 9pm, after which colonel Nic gave us the run down on what was planned for the following day. This would be Saturday, 17th September, the 50th anniversary of the battle of Arnhem. After an early breakfast we were to be taken by coach to Ginkel heath to watch the commemorative parachute drop at 10 am, by British, Canadian and Polish troops, and hopefully, including our 75 Arnhem veterans. Huge crowds were expected so we were to be provided with a picnic lunch. After lunch we would be taken to visit the war cemetery at Oosterbeek. I would have my first opportunity of visiting my father's grave.

I had anticipated that moment many times. Tomorrow it would become an actuality. The sick feeling in my stomach returned. The other guests were talking and eating happily but I felt depressed and cut off and isolated from those around me. I was thankful when dinner was over and Derek and I were able to retire to our room. It was a pleasant, modern room as hotel bedrooms go with an en-suite bathroom and a window overlooking the city. We were both very tired so showered and went straight to bed. I soon fell into an uneasy sleep. My dreams were dark and menacing but when I was awoken by the early morning call I was uncertain of their exact form. Only that they had left me with a darkness of mind and spirit. I struggled mentally to overcome these feeling by thinking about my friend Les Lockett who, along with the other veterans, would be parachuting onto Ginkel heath this morning. I looked out of the window and noticed it was raining hard. The flag on the top of the building opposite was flapping madly in the strong wind.

"The weathers pretty awful," I said to Derek, "I hope the veterans will be able to make their drop."

Derek came across and joined me and we glanced gloomily out on to the rain drenched streets.

"Doesn't look too good," he agreed, "but it's early yet the weather might have improved by 10 o'clock.

The time was just before 7am when we joined the others for breakfast. Colonel Nic informed us that he had heard of the grape vine that the veterans were still hoping to make their drop but the state of play was being monitored by the minute.

After breakfast we were issued with our packed lunches before boarding the coach which would take us to Ginkel heath.

My thoughts returned to that Sunday 50 years ago. The weather on that morning had been misty but later fine and sunny. When the mighty airborne army flew over the coast many people were eating their breakfast or attending church services. Many rushed outside to gaze in wonder at the skies which were alive with the sound of aircraft of every size, some toeing gliders in their wake. How confidently they had flown off to Arnhem. With D-day behind them they intended to capture the bridges opening the way for the advancing allied army. The war would be over by Christmas, that was for sure.

And what was my father, Sergeant Bertie White thinking watching that first wave of paratroopers leaving for Arnhem? Was he impatient for the tomorrow, whiling away the hours, his last hours on this earth? Did his thoughts turn to Rosie, his girl and my mother? Was it to her he wrote his last letter home? Question., More and more questions the answers to which I shall never know.

Leaving Nimegan the coach drive drove out into the Dutch countryside. Passing the woods were the Airborne army came up against the notorious German SS Panzer division in a desperate struggle. The trees were packed closely together and in my imagination I saw their ghostly figures moving silently, stealthily, between the trees. And the dead, laying exposed, unseeing, uncaring now.

The road to Ginkel heath was lined with coaches. I saw several from the British Legions and others from the Arnhem veterans association. I made a mental note to make enquires about traveling with them if I came to Arnhem in the future.. The Dutch people themselves were much in evident. A shuttle bus service was unloading families on their day out.

The heath was much larger than I had imagined; a vast open landscape, as far as the eye could see. Our coach driver put us down half way along the heath with the vague promise of picking us up at lunch time, then disappeared in a sea of coaches. Fortunately the rain had stopped and the wind had dropped to a hopeful degree.

Once on our own Derek and I were out of sight of our companions in a throng of people heading for a vantage viewing points along the heath. It was a relief to be away from the others whose presence at such a time would have seemed intrusive. Here, in the crowd of Dutch people, we could remain anonymous.

The red beret, past and present, was much in evidence. The young paratroopers were here with their regiment to organize the event. The veterans were kings for the day, wearing their red berets and a string of medals with pride. They were old now, many infirm, some confined to wheelchairs, yet there was a steeliness about them. They could afford to hold their heads high among men. They had fought at Arnhem. Today they came to Arnhem to honour their dead and to accept the homage due to them as living heroes. I watched them mingling in the crowd, children scrambling to get their autographs, younger soldiers saluting them, and listened as, in hushed tones, they recounted their stories of the battle so long ago.

Derek and I found a place next to a Dutch family where we had a good view of the heath. We waited patiently as occasionally a light aircraft flew over the heath spewing out a few parachutists. These were greeted good humouredly and with enthusiasm by the waiting crowed. Then, just as my watch read 10 o'clock, we heard a distant rumbling in the sky.

Flying into view, came the huge Deckota, work horse of the sky. She was also a veteran of the war, but powerful still. For a moment the plane seemed to poise over the heath, almost stopping, then the door opened, and out they came, tumbling from the sky in perfect symmetry. For an instant they fell, then their parachutes opened, and they glided down onto the heath. We cheered, then once again, we heard the distant rumbling.

There were four of them in all; unloading with human cargo in the sky. .How did it feel, that moment when they hung between heaven and earth? How did my father feel that day seeing the burning heath come up to meet him? Hearing the firing of the German guns. At what precise moment did the bullets find their mark?

The paratroopers had all landed safely; unhitching themselves, scrambling to their feet, For a moment silence descended on the crowd not knowing what to expect next. Then the air was filled with the sound of thunder as the four huge aircraft circled the heath in convey, then circled again, dipping their wings in salutation to the fallen. It was an intensely moving moment, before they vanished from our sight and the spell was broken. The show was over.

Time passed and the crowd began to disperse. Somewhere along the heath the Prince of Wales was awaited to unveil a new memorial. We did not bother to find out where. Lost in our own thoughts, we walked down the road that runs past the heath. Soon it would be time to find our coach that would take us to the next stop on our pilgrimage. To the war cemetery at Oosterbeek.

***

It is not far!

The journey from Ginkel heath to Oosterbeek.

CHAPTER TEN

It took some hours for the crowd to disperse and the traffic to move freely once more. Well past the time our coach driver had said he would pick us up.

The rain had returned and we were wet, cold and hungry and our paced lunches were still on the coach. Eventually we came upon a small crowd of people wearing the 'Holts' orange badge and who I recognized from our party and so we joined them. Everyone we spoke to was moaning about the lack of organization but, to be fair, it would have been impossible to have kept to a timetable on such an occasion.

Four Holts' coaches passed us, none of them ours, we were almost giving up hope when we spotted our driver pulling up further down the road and we dashed down to meet the coach. All bad feeling was soon abated at the prospect of warmth and food.

I was so glad to get out of the rain I momentarily forgot we were heading for the war cemetery at Oosterbeek. If was Colonels Nic's voice over the loudspeaker system that reminded me. I was about to see my father's grave. The reality of the situation hit me and the food I was eating stuck in my throat. I felt physically sick. Pushing my food aside I tried to concentrate on something else. I found my camera, opened it, and attempted to put a new film in but for some reason the film stuck and would not wind on. I began to get upset because I thought I would not be able to take any photos of my father's grave. Looking back I can see the whole incident was completely out of proportion; it was just a way of directing my mind away from the panic I felt inside.

It didn't take long to drive to Oosterbeek.

Colonel Nic was pointing out places of significance at the time of the battle. It went over my head. All I remember is the tree lined avenue that leads to the war cemetery. The coach pulled to a halt and my stomach turned to ice. I felt as if I had lost the use of my hands and feet. Colonel Nic was telling us we had half an hour to look round and people began to leave their seats.

"I can't do this," I whispered urgently to Derek as people thronged into aisle, eager to get off the coach.

"Come on," said Derek, "you will be all right once you get outside."

The coach was emptying fast. Derek helped me up and I was surprised to discover my legs were still capable of supporting me. Anne, the Colonel's lady, stood at the coach door, waiting for us to get off. It was the look of sympathy in her eyes that finally got me out of the coach. I wasn't prepared to make a fool of myself and shame my father for anyone.

We entered the main gates of the cemetery.

Looking down the rows of graves I could see the huge stone memorial cross at the far end. In the centre there is an open area used to seat the public during services. Already the preparation for tomorrow's service, which Prince Charles and Queen Beatrice would attend, were in progress. The graves surround this central area.

It is a peaceful place, large oak trees mark the boundaries; roses and flowers planted among the graves. Close together they lie in silent companionship. The headstones, all the same, give the rank, name and number of the deceased and, at the foot of the stone, a personal inscription chosen by the next of kin.

"Where do we start," asked Derek, " have you any idea where he is buried."

I rummaged in my bag for the letter from the War Graves Commission.

" Plot 5, row B, grave 10," I read.

"This is plot 7," said Derek surveying the nearest marker, "I think we need to move further down."

We walked towards the memorial cross.

"Can you see the number of this plot?" I asked.

"It's plot 5, the grave must be around here."

I looked down at the grave nearest to me. It was grave 10 in row B. I read the inscription 'Sergeant Bertie White, 156 Battalion, Parachute Regiment. I was standing directly over my father's grave.

"It's here. This is my father's grave."

We stood silently looking down at the headstone. Like all the others, it was inscribed with his rank, name, and number ; over which were the wings, symbol of the Parachute Regiment. I knelt down to see what was written at the foot of the grave, the inscription chosen by his next of kin. It read;

'Greater love have no man

than to lay down his life

for his friend'

Beautiful, simple words from the Gospel of Saint John. Were they, I wondered, chosen by my grandparents?

Derek handed me the small wooden cross with the poppy attached, made by the British Legion.

I pushed the pointed end into the ground.

And, at that very moment, it was as if a force came up to meet me, surrounding me; embracing me; taking me to itself.

Time and space; life and death ceased to exist.

Fear melted from me. I knew there was nothing to be afraid of in this place. It was only my father's poor body that lay in the grave. His spirit was free. It was where it had always had been, always would be, with me. I was aware of a sense of wholeness, of unity.

I looked up and saw Derek standing in exactly the same position as when he had handed me the cross. The experience had lasted no more than a minute, yet, in that time, something had irrevocably changed within me.

There was no need for words. It was a time for tears, but gentle tears. Silently, and in our own way, we said a prayer for our dead.

We left him then. Walking back among the graves at Oosterbeek. Over one thousand men, flower of the Airborne Forces, are buried there. On either side of my father lie paratroopers from his own Battalion, killed on the same day. Sergeant William Walsey, Private Sidney Irons, Colonel William Leach; and their Commanding Officer, Sir William Des Voeux. Once comrades in battle, now comrades in death.

Slowly, stopping now and then to read an inscription on a grave, we made our way to rejoin our party on the coach. Tomorrow Derek and I would return alone for the 50th commemorative service of the battle of Arnhem.

SERGEANT BERTIE WHITE - PARACHUTE REGIMENT
GRAVE TO THE LEFT

CHAPTER ELEVEN

Sunday the 18th September 1994. The 50th anniversary of the second parachute drop on Arnhem; and of my father's death.

The weather was much improved and I was up early washing my hair and getting myself ready. I wanted to look my best. I intended to wear my smart grey suit and bright red jumper. This was to be a very special day and I wanted to honour the occasion.

To me it seemed as if I had been invited, as if my father had waited all those years for this day. By some miracle I was here. This was only one of many such perfectly timed coincidences that I was to encounter during the following months.

Today, as his daughter, I was to represent Sergeant Bertie White, a hero of Arnhem. I felt strongly, that above all, he wanted me to be proud. Proud of his courage. Proud to be his daughter. As indeed I was. My grief, always near the surface, must take second place today.

The road from Oosterbeek to the war cemetery was closed to traffic so we walked down the pleasant tree line road. Large oak trees surround the cemetery and I stopped to pick up a few acorns and out them in my pocket as a memento of the day. When, later I returned home, I planted them in a put in the garden where already they have begun to grow.

We arrived with plenty of time to spare. The Parachute Regiment, past and present, were once again, very much in evidence. The young soldier on duty at the main date directed us to a large marquee where we could pick up our tickets. I explained who I was to the Dutch official behind the counter.

"Have you proof of identification?" he asked kindly.

I pointed to the Holt's name badge I was wearing.

Satisfied he smiled, "one moment please."

He went and spoke to another man. I did not understand what they were saying but the second man nodded and went a way to find something. He returned in a few moments carrying a small blue box. Then holding out his hand he shook my hand warmly.

"Please accept this commemorative medal on behalf of your father with gratitude from the Dutch people," he said warmly.

"Thank you," I replied somewhat bewildered.

I opened the box and found inside a beautiful 50th anniversary commemorative medal. Trying desperately not to cry I pinned it to the collar of my grey suit. It was a proud moment.

Already many people had taken their seats in the cemetery. But the first thing I intended to do was place the silk flowers I had bought from home on my father's grave. I would have much preferred real flowers but these had been easier to transport.

My mood had changed completely from the day before. Now I felt only pride and love as I knelt to lay my flowers on Bertie's grave.

An elderly lady stood watching me. "Was he your dad dear?" she asked sympathetically.

"Yes....but I never knew him."

I noticed she was standing at the grave next to my father's.

"He was my elder brother," she nodded at the headstone.

The grave belonged to Sergeant William Walsey, also of the 156 Battalion, killed at the same time as my father.

"They died at the same time."

"Bloody terrible waste," she said with feeling, "my parent's never got over Bill's death."

I sighed, "yes, it was a terrible waste of life."

She reached out and touched my arms and for an instant we were united in the futility of war.

Derek and I found seats as near as possible to where Bertie was buried. Two brothers from Shropshire sat next to me. They had driven over on the spur of the moment to be at the service. Their father, another Arnhem veteran, had died a few months earlier.

"Dad came ever year, never missed one," the elder brother told me. "He was really looking forward to the 50th." I don't know why but after he died we felt we had to come in his place."

"Did you have difficulty finding somewhere to say," I asked.

"We're staying at the local youth hostel," he grinned, "it's cheap and the food is very good."

There was a feeling of mutual empathy with all those I met that morning. The veterans, the war widows, the children of those who had died. Their mutual sorrow was tangible even after all those years.

It was a very moving service. Prince Charles and Queen Beatrice of the Netherlands were there to represent their countries. The priest who led the service had been a padre at the Battle of Arnhem. General Hackett, commander of the 4th Parachute Brigade, gave an address. He was one of the few commanding officers still alive today. He looked small and unsteady, clutching s walking stick, as he stood up to speak to the congregation. My father would have known him when he was young, I thought sadly.

As if reading my thoughts General Hackett said, "we are all in the dropping zone now."

The military band began to play the hymn 'Abide with me'. The congregation valiantly tried to sing the words but the emotion was too much for many. I saw an elderly lady in front of me, she was clutching a teddy bear sporting a red beret, as she wept uncontrollably. Many of the veterans were blowing their noses or wiping their eyes. Next to me the find strong voice of the man from Shropshire took up the words. I smiled and tried to join him as his voice soared above the crowd.

Once the service was over it was time for the officials to lay their wreaths on the war memorial.

Then it was time for the children to lay their flowers.

It is a custom that children from local schools lay flowers on the war graves each year. The history of the German occupation of their country and their liberation by the allies is taken very seriously in Dutch schools. The children are taught to remember, with gratitude, those who gave their lives at Arnhem.

There were over one thousand children, each carrying a bouquet of flowers. It was a comforting thought that every year there had been someone to lay flowers on my father's grave.

It was then I saw the girl in the wheelchair.

She looked about 12 years of age. Dressed in school uniform like all the others. In fact it was her sameness that first stuck me. She looked bright and happy, chatting with her friends. Only the wheelchair singled her out as being different. And that seemed unimportant. My thoughts returned to Chloe. The specialists all agreed she was intelligent and had much potential. Perhaps if in ten years time she would look like this girl. Suddenly the girl in the wheelchair seemed like a symbol of hope. My spirits lifted.

The children were beginning to disperse around the cemetery, finding the grave they had been allocated to lay flowers on. The girl and her classmates were heading for the graves on our side. I saw Derek look in her direction.

"Do you see that girl in the wheelchair?" he said.

"I've been watching her."

"She looks o.k. doesn't she?" he said reflecting my own thoughts.

The girl came nearer and I heard Derek catching his breath.

"Do you think........"

The girl stopped in front of my father's grave.

"I don't believe it," said Derek in amazement.

The tears I had promised not to shed were unstoppable now.

But it was a magical moment. For to us, this little girl in her wheelchair was a symbol of hope. A sign of recognition from my father. Not only was he watching over us but he understood our worries about Chloe. In his own way he was telling us that it wasn't the end of the world. His great granddaughter Chloe would be o.k.

THE GIRL IN THE WHEELCHAIR WHO PUT FLOWERS ON BERTIE'S GRAVE

CHAPTER TWELVE

The service was over and it would soon be time to leave. Yet I was reluctant to go. I had found an inner peace in this place and now I needed time to be alone here, to come to terms with all I had experienced.

We lingered until it was relatively quiet and then I made my way for the last time to take leave of my father. Strange that only yesterday I had been so afraid. Now my heart ached to stay a while. I felt so much for this man and yet I knew very little about him. I didn't even know what he had looked like I had only a name and a grave.

"I will be back next year, I promise," I said looking down at the head stone. "I will come every year at this time for as long as I am able."

Then, turning away, I forced myself to leave. Tomorrow we had to return home but next year I would find some other way of returning to Arnhem.

But our visit was not yet over and there was still a surprise in store.

Holt's had arranged an afternoon visit to the Hartenstein Airborne Museum. The museum is housed in what was the Hartenstein hotel, where Major General Urquart made his headquarters during the Battle of Arnhem. Today the museum houses a collection of weapons, uniforms, photographs and other memorabilia from the battle.

It is a surprisingly small building and by the time we arrived with our party it was overflowing with visitors. We pushed our way in with the crowd. At times it was almost impossible to get near the exhibits. We were thinking of calling it a day when Derek spotted the photographs on display in the entrance hall. They were very ordinary group photos showing various parachute battalions in 1944. Just rows and rows of paratroopers. The sort of photograph taken routinely to this day. What made the bottom photo so interesting to us was the caption underneath. It read ' Sergeant's Mess 156 Battalion Parachute Regiment June 1944. I stared at it in amazement, for surely I must be looking at a photograph of my father.

I knelt down to get a closer view. People were pushing past and I found it difficult to keep my balance. I wanted a photograph of my father and now, in all probability, I was looking at one. Somewhere, in among those 60 or so men in the photograph surely must be my father.

"It was taken in June 1944 , three months before Arnhem so he must be here somewhere."

We looked more closely for a face that in some way looked familiar. A face that resembled my own. But it was impossible to tell.

"Do you think we might ask one of the museum staff if they have a copy of the photo?" I asked.

"They're all so busy," replied Derek, "I'll try down stairs at the souvenir counter; maybe they have a book with those photographs in."

The souvenir counter was in the basement and was jammed tight with people trying to buy gifts and momentos. It was impossible to even see what was on sale behind the counter. A weary looking sales assistant was valiantly serving the waiting throng.

"We're never going to get to the front of the queue before it's time to leave," I said desperately.

"Let's have a try anyway. I'll wait hear and you go upstairs and keep an eye open for the rest of them and call me when are ready to leave."

Reluctantly I went back up the stairs and once again stared

incredulously at the photograph. 'I just can't leave without finding out if Bertie is in this photo,' I told myself. Several people I recognized from our party passed me on their way out but there were still a few lingering inside. We could afford to wait a little longer. It was almost closing time and an attendant began rounding up people and asking them leave. I decided I had better go and find Derek but when I got down stairs he was nowhere to be seen. The counter staff were closing down and the room was almost deserted.

"The museum is now closing. Will all visitors please make their way to the main entrance," announced an attendant to those of us who remained.

A feeling of panic was taking hold. How could I leave without finding out. Then common sense took over. Now was not the time. I was never going to get anyone to help me today. Better leave now and make enquires later, either by phone or by letter. Having made that decision I joined the stream of people leaving the building.

Derek was already outside frantically trying to get in again to find me. He was very relieved when he saw me.

"Any luck?"

"No. I did get to the front of the queue but there was nothing as far as I could see with the photos in. They were rushed off their feet."

They were locking the main doors behind us and all hope of finding if my father was in the photograph faded. We both felt extremely frustrated. So near and yet so far. Tomorrow we would have to leave Holland and make the journey home. I had to content myself with the promise that as soon as I arrived home I would contact the museum.

It was only later that it began to dawn on me what a miraculous coincidence it had been. Out of all the hundreds of thousands of British, American and Polish troops who took part in the battle of Arnhem that there should, in all probability, be a photograph of Bertie in this tiny museum seemed nothing less than a miracle. Only a few hours before I had wished for a photograph of my father. Another of those coincidences that defy explanation.

***

Monday morning and it was time to pack up and leave. I felt a desperate urge to stay for a few more days. To let the coach go without me. I needed to remain here when all the visitors had left. To walk on the heath where my father had died. To wander through the woods where the Airborne Army had held out. To visit alone the cemetery where silently they lay.

It was not to be.

Like a docile puppet I boarded the coach for home. Colonel Nic was in good form all the way, keeping up a running commentary on all the places we passed of the slightest interest to the military minded amongst us. Behind me a large man talked incessantly, in a loud voice, about the atrocities carried out on the Jews in the concentrations camps. He was quite an authority. Mile after mile of endless motorway. But my heart and mind were still at Arnhem.

At last we arrived in Calais in time to board the ferry for England. Soon we would be home.

Our pilgrimage to Arnhem was completed.

CHAPTER THIRTEEN

One of my first tasks on returning home was to write to the Hartenstein Airborne Museum, which I did, and posted it the very next day. I was thrilled when I received the following reply.

Airborne Museum

Hartenstein

Oosterbeek

18th October 1994

Dear Mrs Susan Arrowsmith

Thank you for your moving letter of 21st September. I have asked our photographer to make a copy of the photograph you mentioned with our compliments.

I shall try and find if your father is in it. The list I have at home is incomplete. In case I cannot find your father's name I'll give you someone else's address. He might know.

I'll be in touch.

Yours sincerely, Adrian Groenweg, Vice Chairman Board of Trustees

Then, just a week later, I received another letter from Adrian. Inside was a copy of the photograph together with a list of names. The list shown that a Sergeant White was 5th in line from the back row.

Airborne Museum
Hartenstein
Oosterbeek
25th October 1994

Dear Mrs Susan Arrowsmith

Further to my letter of the 18th October I am enclosing a copy of the photograph of the Sergeants Mess of 156 Para Battalion and a list of names I obtained from Major Tony Thomas, an Arnhem Colour Sergeant in the Battalion.

In the back row, right 5 is a Sergeant White. There may have been other Sergeants called White because of course it is quite a common name. Tony Thomas might be able to help you further. The latest address I have for Major T Thomas MBS is...

Mention my name, he might remember me.

Yours sincerely, Adrian

I gazed at the man in the photograph. It showed only his head and shoulders and because the photograph was so small the size of the face was no larger than a five pence piece. I hunted around for my magnifying glass for a closer inspection and this greatly enlarged the image. He wore a beret that covered most of his head so it was impossible to see if his hair was curly like mine. It was a pleasant face, he had been a good looking man. There was a sensitivity about his features, yet at the same time a feeling of strength. I looked more closely and I realised the face was not unfamiliar, the set of the eyes, the shape of the chin were as my own. Whatever Adrian said I knew this man was my father. Later, I did write to Major Thomas to confirm the fact and received the following reply.

Major T Thomas MBE (Para)

Camberley

Surrey

6th November 1994

Dear Mrs Arrowsmith

Thank you for your letter and yes I did know your father he was a good man and an excellent soldier he is the one in the photograph. You can be justly proud of him.

I have put a little bit in my newsletter to the veterans of the Battalion and will let you know what I find about him.

Yours sincerely, Tony Thomas

Sadly, Major Thomas was unable to trace anyone else who remembered my father. I was to find out more about him in quite a different way, but in the meantime I was more than pleased to have confirmation that the man in the photograph was Sergeant Bertie White.

When Derek saw the photograph he suggested that we take it to a professional photographer and have the portion of the photo that showed my father enlarged. We looked through the Yellow Pages and I picked a studio that said they specialized in copying old photographs.

We called in on the next Saturday morning and noticed that it was a small family business. A pleasant middle aged lady came to our assistance and I explained our mission.

"This is the only photo I have of my father," I explained, "and if it's possible I would like to have the part of the photograph that contains his image to be enlarged so that I have a reasonably clear head and shoulders photo."

She scrutinized the photograph carefully through a magnifying glass.

"That should be no problem although the photo will lose some of its details with enlarging I am sure we can make a pretty good job of it for you."

I was struck by the fact that she spoke with a strong foreign accent that sounded familiar.

"Your accent sounds familiar," I ventured.

She smiled, "My home was in Holland but I moved to Norfolk with my husband after we were married."

"We have recently come home from a pilgrimage to the war cemetery at Oosterbeek in Holland, where my father is buried," I explained.

"Ah, yes Arnhem," she said sympathetically, "this photo must be very precious to you?"

"It is but I am sure you will take good care of it."

It was comforting to leave the photograph with someone who understood. Just as we were about to leave a large brown and white spaniel lumbered over to greet us. I bent down to stroke his silky head.

"Get down Bertie," she said to the dog good humouredly, "he likes to greet everyone who comes into the shop.

I met Derek's eyes over the top of the dogs head and we smiled knowing what each other was thinking. A lady from Holland who understood about Arnhem, a dog called Bertie. Another of those unexplained coincidences.

***

A couple of weeks later we went back to the studio to collect my photograph. The photographer had made a fair copy of my father's head and shoulders and now I could see, without the aid of a magnifying glass, how he had looked just a few months before he died.

We purchased a silver frame and today it stands on a shelf in my study where I can see it as I work. Often, as I look up he appears to be watching me. Sometimes, when I am worried or depressed, I tell him my problems and I feel the easier for it.

CHAPTER FOURTEEN

The months that followed our pilgrimage to Arnhem were difficult ones for me. Inevitably, facing the reality of my father's death had taken an emotional toll on me. It was as if I were mentally stuck in a time warp. I was experiencing the grief of bereavement in much the same way as if were 1944.

By October I was losing ground fast and I knew I was spiralling downwards into the darkness of depression. Turning the radio on and catching a certain melody had me dissolving in tears. The haunting lines of a William Owen war poem went round and round in my head. The falling leaves of autumn and the shorter darker days mirrored the shadows of my mind. Inevitably I was forced to seek help from doctor Kitson.

"I don't think its medication you need," said my doctor, "I think some talking therapy with a bereavement counselor would be beneficial to you at this stage."

"Yes, I have been thinking along those lines," I agreed.

"In that case I will give you a leaflet about the Norwich Center and you can give them a ring to make an appointment and tell them that I sent you."

A week later found me knocking on the door of an old Victorian house opposite the Roman Catholic cathedral in Norwich. I had an appointment with a Mrs Meadow and it was she who came down the stairs to greet me. She looked to me to be in her mid-thirties and was pleasant to look at, with her pale freckled face and reddish hair which she wore long cascading over her shoulders. She wore a coloured tank top and a long peasant style skirt, which surprised me as I had expected someone more formally dressed.

She ushered me into her consulting room which had a large window overlooking the cathedral. After the formalities and form filling were completed she asked me to tell her in my own words the reasons why I had come to see her. I can't remember exactly what I said during that first session only that I found that I could talk to her easily. She had a way of listening attentively and at the same time remaining almost motionless so as not to disturb my train of thought. When I paused to think she often echoed my own thoughts as if she were sharing them with me.

At the end of first session I realised that the grief I felt for my father was only some of the negative emotions I was experiencing. I was also very angry. Angry with my mother. My father had laid in his grave for 50 years and in all those years she had kept her secret from me. But mother was dead and I had no way of releasing these strong emotions. She was beyond my reach. At this point Mrs Meadows concluded the session and we arranged to meet again the following Friday.

At the second session I took with me the photograph of Bertie, now set in its silver frame. We set it down on the small table between us and here it remained for all our future sessions.

"He is so much part of my life now and yet I know so little about him." I explained. "It is as if there is a void in my mind. As if part of my identity is missing and only by discovering my father's history can I find out who I really am."

Mrs Meadows looked at the photograph and smiled, "It's odd but while you were talking I could sense him in the room with you as if he were giving you his courage."

"I feel that way quite often," I confessed, " It is as if he is watching over me and that was why I had no hesitation in coming to see you. I knew he would find me the right therapist. Someone who would understand."

Looking back I have no doubt that these counselling sessions helped me to turn a corner and gain a greater understanding of my own feelings. It was a time of finding my strengths and understanding my vulnerabilities. It was not all plain sailing and some Fridays I would leave the center feeling bleak indeed. Yet she was always there with me to comfort me and help me to think more positively about the future.

Even so these was one particular weekend when I felt particularly low in spirits. I remember going to the little Catholic church I liked to attend on most Sundays and feeling deeply depressed. The theme of the service on that particular Sunday morning was the survival of the spirit after death. A phrase from one of the psalms stuck in my mind. 'At night there are tears, but joy comes with the morning.' In the days that followed I could not get it out of my head. Somehow the words seemed to have a message for me. I imagined that it meant that when I had passed through this time of darkness I would find the joy of the morning. I hung on to this thought and gradually as the days passed I reached an equilibrium.

November came bringing with it the birth of our second granddaughter Holly. A few days after Holly's birth I travelled to Kent to spend a week with my daughter Samantha and her new baby. It was a moment of great joy when I held my beautiful granddaughter for the first time. How wonderful that my father's genes lived on in this new child.

By Christmas my counselling sessions with Mrs Meadows were drawing to an end. I had talked a great deal about my mother. I tried to imagine how her life must have been before I was born. She was in her early twenties and already a war widow with a young daughter when she fell pregnant with her lover's child. Yet, she had not taken the easy way out and had an abortion. She had chosen to give birth to me. How would I have coped in a similar situation? Not half so well. True, she had kept the secret of my father from me and I still felt this was wrong. But I no longer stood in judgment over her, instead I felt a pity for her that I had never felt during her life time.

One day when I was clearing out the spare bedroom I found the photograph Dad had given to me of my mother taken when they were first married. I placed it on a shelf in my study. Some weeks later some impulse made me place it next to the photograph of Bertie.

"Why don't you buy her a silver frame to match your father's," asked Derek?

"I don't think I'm ready to go that far," I laughed.

But the following Saturday we went into Norwich to buy another silver frame. Today these photographs stand together on the shelf above my desk. There is also a third photo of a tiny child that stands with them. To the casual observer we look like a happy family, soldier daddy, smiling mother and impish child. But, of course, we were never a real family, we never had the chance to be, and I can only dream of how it might have been, if my daddy had come home from the war.

SERGEANT BERTIE WHITE   **ROSE BUCKLEY**

PART THREE

IRELAND

CHAPTER FIFTEEN

The New Year of 1995 came and with it my thoughts returned to my promise to return to Arnhem in September. Finances were a problems so I contacted the 'Lest we forget society', to enquire about the possibility of traveling with the Arnhem veterans on their annual pilgrimage. They were quick to reply enclosing the address of Mrs Marion Walpole who lives in Norfolk and for many years has arranged an annual pilgrimage for the veterans and the next of kin of those who died at Arnhem. Marion proved to be most helpful and was happy to include me and Derek in her coach party for September.

With the Arnhem pilgrimage booked for another year I could safely turn my attention to other matters. Since our aborted visit to St. Catherine's House, when we failed to trace my father's birth certificate, I had decided to write to the Registrar of births, marriages and deaths in Dublin. I sent as much information as I had gleaned during my research but my request for a birth certificate was turned down because I had insufficient information. I then had two choices, either I employ a genealogist in Dublin to search the records on my behalf, or, Derek and I would travel to Ireland and search the records ourselves.

We decided to go to Ireland ourselves.

Having made the decision we spent some time in discussing when and where to go. We decided on the month of April because, apart from the fact that it would be cheaper then, the roads are quieter and the countryside is especially beautiful in the spring. We decided on a self catering package holiday and when I was browsing through the Stena Sealink brochure I came across a holiday report in Co. Tyrone, Northern Ireland. Immediately I knew this was where we should go. It wasn't anything particular about the resort itself that was so appealing. It was just a feeling I had inside.

"How about going to Co. Tyrone?", I suggested to Derek.

"Co Tyrone is in Northern Ireland and I thought you wanted to go to Dublin to visit the record office," he said doubtfully.

"I do but that doesn't mean we have to stay in Dublin our research is unlikely to take long so we can drive over the border for a day or two at the most."

"Have you thought about the troubles in Northern Ireland?"

"The cease fire has lasted for months now so we are unlikely to be in an any danger."

But thinking it over I had to admit Derek was right there was no point in staying in Northern Ireland when the purpose of our visit was to search the records in Dublin. There was no logical reason why we should go to Co. Tyrone but still I could not rid myself of the voice in my head that was telling me to do just that. In the event we decided on a self-catering holiday in Killykeen, Co. Caven, midway between Dublin and Co. Tyrone.

The following morning we drove to the travel agents in Diss to book our holiday. For some reason I felt tense and irritable. After weeks of counselling I felt in control of my life once more. Would Ireland prove to be as traumatic as Arnhem? By making this journey would I, once again, be stepping onto an emotional roller-coaster?

Once in the travel agents we sat balancing on those ridiculous high stalls while the girl called up the accommodation, availability dates and sailing times on her computer.

"Do you want to sail on the ferry or would you prefer the catamaran?"

We looked at each other uncertainly.

"The catamaran is faster but costs £15 extra each way," she added.

"Let's pay extra and go on the catamaran," said Derek, "it will save time."

"Please yourself," I said unenthusiastically.

Back in the car I felt near to tears. We had booked to go to Ireland in a months time and I didn't want to go.

"What's wrong?" asked Derek.

"I don't know....I suppose I'm scared".

"It's a bit late to feel scared...I've just paid for the holiday, in cash."

"I've got this horrible feeling," I said as I wept into a tissue.

He looked at me in exasperation. "Look at it this way," he said at last, "you have to find out about your father, you said so yourself, and the only way you can find out is to go to Ireland. It doesn't matter how much it costs, or, what it takes, you have to go for you own piece of mind."

And, of course, he was right. I knew in my heart that I would travel to the end of the earth if needs be.

When we had finished our errand in Diss we decided to drive on into Banham where there is a craft center, in an ancient barn, that I enjoying visiting. I am an avid collector of glass animals and they always have a good selection made by a local craftsman. My collection dates back to when I was 16 when they were much in fashion. At the time I was fascinated by a friend's collection. Today I have a vast collection kept in a display cabinet but I am always on the look out for something unusual, although with so many glass animals of my own it is difficult to find something different.

Today, my mind was only half interested as we stared through the window at the current display. I wasn't anticipating finding anything unusual. At the same moment our eyes alighted on the glass Pegasus.

"Look at that," I said excitedly, "It's Pegasus. I've never seen one of those before."

"So it is! the mythological winged horse."

"Pegasus is the emblem of the Paratroop Regiment," I told him.

"Then, it must be a good sign."

"Let's buy the Pegasus, it may bring us luck."

We hurried round to the barn door only to be disappointed to find that the craft center had already closed for the day.

"We'll come back tomorrow," promised Derek.

There was nothing further we could do so we drove home. My mood had lifted considerably from the morning and I was actually looking forward to going to Ireland. The words of the psalm came into my head. 'At night there are tears, but joy comes with the morning.' Arnhem had been a time for tears, maybe, I would find my joy in the morning in Ireland?

***

When we returned to Banham craft center the following morning the Pegasus had already been sold. Not to be beaten Derek asked for the telephone number of the craftsmen who made the glass animals. When we spoke to him he was happy to make me another. Today this Pegasus holds pride of place in my collection.

CHAPTER SIXTEEN

During the weeks that preceded our visit to Ireland I had two vivid dreams that I felt were important. These were the type I now recognized as prophetic dreams. They differ from other dreams in that I am always aware that I am asleep and it is as if I am watching myself act out the dream but, at the same time, also taking part in the dream and experiencing all the emotion.

The first dream was short and repeated over several nights. I saw myself gazing out over a large expanse of water. It was so vast I could easily have been looking out to sea. There were waves on the surface of the water but somehow I knew it was a large lake or lough and this was somewhere my father had often visited.

The second dream was more explicit and it occurred only once. In the Derek and I were together and I knew we were in Ireland. We were standing outside of a house, with several other people who I did not recognize. Someone knocked on the door and it was opened by an old man. The man looked directly at me, and seemed to be expecting us because he smiled and excitedly ushered us all inside. I followed the others into a small hall that led into the living room and a kitchen beyond. He held out his hand to me. As I took his hand I looked into his face. He was old, about the same age as my father would have been had he lived, I could see a strong resemblance to the photograph I had of Bertie. It was as if I were looking at my father in old age.

I puzzled a great deal over this second dream and what it may mean. I came to the conclusion that my father could have had a brother and it might be him I saw in my dream. But if so, where was he? I could only wait and see.

We were booked to sail on the Stena Sealink catamaran from Holyhead to Dublin on the 22nd April. The drive to Holyhead was over three hundred miles so we decided to leave very early in the morning to get there in plenty of time for the 5.30pm sailing.

Our son David and his wife Heather, who had offered to stay at our house while we were away, to look after our numerous birds and animals, arrived in time for dinner on Friday evening. We sat down for our last meal together before we set out on the next stage of our mission.

"This time tomorrow you will be in Ireland, the home of our ancestors," said David.

"Yes," I replied thoughtfully, "let's hope I find some of the ancestors still living."

"Where do you intend to start?"

"With the Registrar of births, marriages and deaths in Dublin. The first step is to search the records for my father's birth certificate. It should be relatively easy as we know how old he was when he died in September 1944, and that his parents were Abraham and Elizabeth. Then we can search the records of marriages for my grandparent's marriage certificate. These will give me the place where my father was born and where my grandparents were living before they married.

"Sounds exciting."

"Yes," I said cautiously, "the only problem is, if Dublin is anything like St Catherine's House, I will have to wait a week for the copies of the certificates. By that time we shall be home in England."

"You should have booked for longer."

"Maybe. But the indexes will give the district where the entries were registered," I replied.

"What then?"

"It is possible my father had brothers and sisters, some of whom may be still alive.

"Once you find the district you could look up all the Whites in the telephone directory," suggested Derek.

"I could," I said thoughtfully, "but I don't intend to approach people in that way.....no surprise! surprise! element."

"It's the easiest way."

"No, that's not my way. I remember how I felt when Dad had knocked on my door that morning. A person needs time to take in news like that. What I intend to do is advertise in the local newspaper for friends and relatives of my father. That way they can choose to answer, or not, if they don't wish to own me."

We laughed and the subject was dropped. I thought how it might feel if I really did discover some of my father's family. But I realised it was a remote possibility. Had he lived my father would have been 80 years of age and the only lead I had was the area where he was born. Any remaining relatives, in all probability, would have moved from that area many years ago. And yet, sometimes families remained in the same area for generations.

The morning we left for Ireland was dark and gloomy and it was raining hard. The car was packed tightly with every conceivable item we might need for a weeks self catering, plus two days rations in case the shops were closed on Sunday in Southern Ireland. My final item of packing was my father's photograph which I placed carefully in the top of my make up case.

"Tonight we sleep in Ireland," I promised as I closed the lid.

But that was a promise I was unable to keep.

The journey to Holyhead was remarkably trouble free and we made good progress, by early afternoon we were crossing Stevenson's famous Mennine bridge into Wales. Never having travelled so far west before we were now on unknown territory. The landscape gradually changed from gentle hills and valleys, to wilder, less inhabitable outcrops of land. Huge craggy peaks towered above up. We were in Snowdonia . The sky was grey and overcast. A mist hovered around the summit of the mountains, shrouding them from our sight. I stared heaven ward transfixed by the magnitude of the mountains. On such a day it seemed an awesome place.

At around 3pm we arrived in Holyhead. Time for a meal before we headed for the ferry terminus. Well in time for the 5pm catamaran, or, so we hoped.

The road to the terminus was choked with cars and lorries. It was obvious there would be some delay. Derek abandoned the car and went to discover what was wrong. The catamaran sailing had been cancelled because of severe weather conditions. The ferry was unable to leave the harbour due to a breakdown of the engines.

It was a disappointing end to our journey. We spent the next 5 hours waiting, with several hundred other tired and frustrated passengers, outside the ferry terminus. At around 9.30pm two harassed officials informed the angry crowds that all Sealink sailings were cancelled. I shall not dwell on the scenes that followed. I leave that to the reader's imagination.

Derek turned the car round and we headed desolately back though the town. Eventually we found a room for the night in a small hotel. Numbly, we lugged our suitcases up several flights of stairs to our room. Then, too exhausted to speak, we fell into bed and tried to sleep.

CHAPTER SEVENTEEN

The first thing I was aware of the following morning was the sun shining through a chink in the curtains. It was still early but it was obviously going to be a better day. We had slept reasonably well and our spirits were restored to optimism.

"Let's see if we can get breakfast," I suggested, "then we can drive back to the ferry terminus and see the state of play."

All was silent so we found our way down the stairs to the dining room. A buffet breakfast was laid out so we helped ourselves to fruit juice and cereals. From somewhere round the back a cheerful looking waitress appeared and supplied us with tea and toast.

"Are you with the coach part for the ferry?" she asked.

"No, but we are hoping to cross on the ferry," replied Derek. "Is there any news?"

"Well, we have just had a call from a coach driver who is trying to round up some of his passengers, seems the ferry will be sailing at 9am this morning."

We looked at our watches. Not yet 8am. "Let's finish breakfast and get ourselves down to the ferry," I said joyfully.

We hurriedly packed our bags and paid the bill, then turned the car towards Holyhead.

In contrast to the night before the terminus was almost deserted. As we approached a man looked at our tickets, then waved us ahead. A few minutes later we were safely on board. Finally, at 9am, we sailed for Ireland.

It was a wonderful crossing, the seas was calm and the sun

shining. It was an unscheduled sailing because the ships engines had been successfully repaired during the night. Many of the unfortunate passengers from last night were unaware of the morning's change of fortune. They were probably still laying abed as we set sail. Those of us who were lucky enough to be on board found the ship half deserted.

There was an air of friendly camaraderie among the passengers. We all had horror stories of the night before and to exchange and the time passed extremely pleasantly. By noon the coast of Ireland came into view and I had the first sighting of my father's homeland.

We disembarked at the port of Dun Laoghaire and drove through Dublin. The great city was enjoying a Sunday. a day of rest, with offices and shops closed, the roads were uncharacteristically quiet. Soon, we were leaving the suburbs and heading north for Co. Cavan. It was almost 4 o'clock before we spotted the signs for Killykeen Forest. Turning onto a B road we encountered the hazards of driving on minor roads in Southern Ireland. Pot holes. Huge craters littered the road and Derek juggled with the steering wheel as he attempted to avoid the holes.

"This is more like an obstacle course than a road," I said.

"Just as well we didn't have to drive down here in the dark."

The road continued in the same fashion for several miles and it was with relief that we eventually reached the entrance of Killykeen Forest Park.

But it was all well worth it. The forest was enchanting, huge trees fresh in their springtime finery and the ground carpeted with wild primroses, celandines and sweet smelling violets. We parked the car and walked down towards the lake where, overlooking the lake, a row of cedar wood cabins had been built. The air was fresh and clear and we breathed in deeply savouring the moment. Apart from a few fishermen down by the water we were alone.

"I hope we can find the key," I said when we reached our cabin.

"The girl I spoke to on the telephone said she would leave the key inside the bucket."

Sure enough we found the bucket on the porch and inside was the key where she had promised. Once inside, we found the cabin was unexpectedly warm. In anticipation of our late arrival someone had thoughtfully turned the heating on. The cabin was built on two levels with a flight of wooden stairs leading down to the kitchen and living area where a picture window overlooked the late.

"Oh! it's so beautiful," I said thankfully, "and so peaceful."

"Let's unpack and car and find the picnic basket to see if our food is still edible," said Derek.

We found the cool box containing the chicken, cheese and salad, which we had packed early on Saturday morning.

"It's still quite cold," I observed as I lifted the chicken out, "it seems no worse for a night in the back of the car."

We set the table and opened the bottle of wine we had purchased in the duty free shop on the ferry. All was quiet save the last sounds of the birds. The anxiety and frustration of our journey were already receding from our minds.

"Let's drink a toast," said Derek.

"We lifted our glasses.

"To Bertie White," said Derek.

"To Bertie White and home, " I echoed. "Here's to a successful mission."

CHAPTER EIGHTEEN

It was a warm April morning and we woke to the songs of the birds. We decided to have a quiet day to recuperate after the trials of our journey. So, after a leisurely breakfast, we made our way to the site office to tell them we had arrived safely. I also wanted to make enquiries about coach services to Dublin. We decided that if we went by coach we would avoid the harassment of driving in an unknown city and the worry of parking.

The caretaker proved to be polite and helpful.

"Yes, there is a daily coach service to Dublin that leaves from the local pub at 7.30am every weekday morning," he informed us, then warned. "Make sure you get there sharp he waits for no man."

Derek drove up to the pub to make sure we knew exactly where to pick up the coach the next morning. A man was working on one of the coaches and Derek went over to check the time of departure with him.

"Sure," said the man, "coach leaves at 7.30am. Sharp though," he warned.

We got the message and at 7.15am, the following morning, we were waiting outside the pub with a small crowd of regular commuters and a couple of women having a day out at the shops.

The coach driver was leaning nonchalantly against the pub door talking to whoever happened to pass by. At 7.29am he leapt into the driving seat, gave a cursory glance at the passengers and started the engine. The coach pulled away at 7.30am. Sharp.

Dublin looked very different from the city we had driven through on Sunday morning. The roads were choked with early morning rush hour traffic and the streets teamed with people streaming into the shops and offices.

The Registrar office of Births, Marriages and Deaths proved to be a surprisingly small building. The early records were housed in an office on the second floor. We made our way up the stairs to a counter where a notice informed us that the appropriate form had to be completed before requesting the appropriate indexes.

"You can have up to five indexes at a time," the clerk behind the counter informed us.

"I shall only need the births indexes for year 1913 and 1914," I replied confidently.

"We may as well have five years," said Derek, "just in case........"

I completed the necessary forms requesting details of all births registered in the whole of Ireland for the years 1912 to 1916 and paid the fee of £2.50. A few minutes late five, thick, red bound volumes were thumped down in front of us. We staggered over to a spare table.

"Where do we start?" asked Derek.

"Well, if Bertie was aged 30 when he died in September 1944, he must have been born between September 1913 and September 1914," I explained. "You take 1913 and I'll take 1914. All we have to do is look for a Bertie White, mother Elizabeth and father Abraham, born somewhere in Northern Ireland, there shouldn't be that many."

"This proved to be an overstatement as there were no birth entries for Bertie White registered in Northern Ireland between those dates.

"That's odd," I said, "maybe the age given on the death certificate is wrong."

"Better try the other volumes," said Derek.

We took another volume each and were more successful as there were two entries under the name of Bertie White, both of them in Northern Ireland. The next step was to complete a further request form for a photocopy of the actual entry. This would give us the full names of bother parents.

We waited in happy anticipation until the clerk reappeared bearing our photocopies. Eagerly we scanned through the details. We looked at each other in disbelief. Neither entry gave the patents' names as Abraham and Elizabeth.

"I don't understand," I said sadly, "he must be here somewhere."

I sat deep in thought trying to make sense of the situation. Either the date or name on my father's death certificate must be incorrect. Now what might Bertie be short for, I mused?

I had an idea. "Perhaps Bertie is short for Albert," I suggested.

"Could be," conceded Derek, "lets go back to the beginning and look for all the Albert's born between 1913 and 1914."

There were quite a few entries for Albert, it seemed to have been a popular name of the time. Of all those registered in Northern Ireland we obtained photocopies. Each time proved to be a disappointment. When the final entry proved to be a dud I felt the panic rising. I remembered our fruitless search at St. Catherine's house, surely this could not be a repeat performance.

"All we can do now is extend our search," I said unhappily.

"I'll pay for another five years," said Derek.

We went to the desk and handed over our forms and money and a short time later we staggered back under the weight of another five volumes. Occasionally, we came on an entry that sounded promising only to be frustrated when the clerk appeared with the photocopy. Finally we came to the end of the last volume.

"Nothing," said Derek in despair.

I covered my face with my hands my mind in confusion. Surely we hadn't come all this way to Ireland on a wild goose chase. If only I could still my mind I knew I would find the answer but I was too agitated to think clearly. 'Bertie, help me,' I pleaded silently.

"Robert," said Derek breaking into my thoughts.

"What do you mean?" I said, unable to see the connection.

"Bertie can be short for Robert."

"Can it?" I thought about this for a moment. "You may be right, anyway it's worth a try. Let's go back to 1913 and 1914."

There were several Roberts registered in Southern Ireland but it was May 1914 before I came upon the first promising entry.

"Robert White registered in Coalisland, Dungannon," I read aloud. "Is Dungannon in Northern Ireland?" I asked.

"Yes, Coalisland if often mentioned on the news. It's been one of the flash points in the recent troubles."

"It a possible then," I replied, "better find another £1.50 for the man."

Derek made another trip to the desk while I carried on searching the records. I found another entry for September 1914. "I may as well get this one," I said when Derek returned. "It will be lunch time soon and the offices closes for an hour until 2.30."

It was my turn to pay so I joined the queue of people waiting for attention. A few minutes later I heard Derek calling me as he excitedly waved a piece of paper.

"I've got it," he said jubilantly.

"It's o.k.," I beamed at the clerk, "we have found what we were looking for..."

Our relief was tangible. I could easily have wept as I gazed at the entry. 'Robert White born in Dungannon, Co. Tyrone, May 1913, parents Elizabeth (formerly Graham) and Abraham White." It was true we had found Bertie.

"We have cracked it," I laughed, "Bertie was short for Robert."

We sat grinning stupidly at each other over the enormous pile of red volumes.

"Let's get these back and then we can apply for a full birth certificate," suggested Derek. "We should have time before they close for lunch."

We were relieved to learn that, after paying a fee of £5.50, we could collect the birth certificate that morning. I sat in a happy daze waiting for our number to come up on the display indicator when our certificate was ready for collection. For a time this morning it has seemed as if we had come to a dead end. Now we had our first lead towards finding my father's family.

Our number came up on the display and Derek collected the certificate. We spread it out on the desk. 'Robert White born at Drumkee, father Abraham White residing at Derrywinner, mother Elizabeth White (nee Graham), date of birth.......'

"My God!" I exclaimed in astonishment. "Look at the date of Bettie's birth....."

"26th May 1914," read Derek, "our wedding anniversary."

We looked at each and laughed and I though back to the year of our marriage. The original date had been set for September but we had changed it to the 26th May. Had it been a coincidence?"

"Just think we have been celebrating my father's birthday every year since we were married."

"Odd isn't it," agreed Derek, "another of those strange coincidences."

"Almost as if he were walking down the aisle with me," I replied thoughtfully."

"He probably was."

Then I remembered something our son David has said when we told him my father died at Arnhem on the 18th September 1944. He and Heather had unknowingly married on the same day in 18th September 1993. David had said that there was on real reason why they had chosen that date. It just a date that had come into his head!

We had a quick lunch at McDonalds then spent the remaining time browsing the gift shops for souvenirs to take home. When we returned to the Registrar Office the same man was behind the desk.

I handed him a slip requesting the volumes for marriages recorded between 1910 and 1914 together with the £2.50 fee. I felt like an old hand. This time he gave me five, slimmer, green volumes. Evidently there were far fewer marriages than births recorded during that period.

In less than an hour we were in possession of a copy of my grandparent's marriage certificate. Elizabeth Graham, a dressmaker from Drumkee had married Abraham White, a farmer, from Corrainey on 14th May 1913, at the Second Presbyterian Church in Dungannon.

"So, my grandfather was a farmer and my grandmother a dressmaker," I said musing over the certificate.

"Now you know where you get your green fingers," replied Derek.

"Yes, or course, that's why, even as a child, I was always trying to make things grow. The reason why I have this need to live near green fields."

"What about your grandmother, the dressmaker? Remember all those dressed you have made," Derek reminded me. "If I remember rightly your sewing machine was the first piece of household equipment we brought before we were married."

"So it was," I smiled remembering how, even as a small child, I loved to make clothes for my dolls. Years later I was taught how to make my own clothes at school and became skilled in the art of dressmaking. Skills never possessed by either my mother or my sisters.

It as if pieces of a jigsaw were falling in to place. I was discovering the origins of facets of my character previously unexplained. My forbears on my father's side had probably all been farmers. My roots were deeply entrenched in the countryside. That was why I felt out of place when living in an urban environment.

CHAPTER NINETEEN

With the first part of my mission successfully completed I was ready to turn my mind to my second goal. To visit the place where my father was born and begin the search for any living relatives.

When I broached the subject of travelling to Coalisland the next day, Derek was uncharacteristically reluctant.

"What do you plan to do when you get there?" he asked.

"I don't know," I relied truthfully, "I just want to see the place where my father was born."

"I'm worried about going to Coalisland," he confessed, "the guide books says it has been one on the 'trouble' sports and not recommended for tourists."

"But the cease fire has lasted for more than six months."

"Yes, but you can't just cruise around the back streets of Coalisland without any clear idea of where you want to go. It would look suspicious."

"I want to go to the places mentioned on the certificate, Drumkee and Derrywinner."

"I have had a look on the map but I can't locate them."

"Maybe they are just small parishes..."

"That's what I mean," said Derek in exasperation, "we shall end up driving round and round with no idea where we are going. It is Northern Ireland you know."

I understood why he was reluctant to go to Coalisland. For twenty years the news from Northern Ireland had been dominated with reports of terrorist bombings and sectarian murders. There was always the possibility we could unwittingly get caught up in some violence. But I had this overwhelming compulsion to go to Drumkee and Derrywinner. The idea had taken control of my mind. Nothing else mattered to me. I was drawn inexplicably to those places where my father had spent the early days of his life.

Next morning found us still at odds. I lay in bed tearful and obstinate. I made unrealistic plans in my mind about hiring a car and driving myself to Coalisland, or, pay someone to take me. One thing was certain, I had no intention of leaving Ireland until I had visited Bertie's home.

"Very well," Derek agreed at last, "we'll drive to Enniskillen. We can have lunch there and buy an ordinance survey map which should show Drumkee and Derrywinner. Then we can work out the best route to take."

I didn't want to go to Enniskillen but it was a step in the right direction.

We hardly spoke on the drive to the border check point. Derek drove silently, eyes fixed on the road, me, consumed by a desperation to reach Coalisland, hardly noticed what we passed on the way. Eventually we arrived at the border check point at Swainlinbar and saw that it was deserted. It had he eerie look of an abandoned film set, barriers open but no sign of life from the fortified viewing tower, with the close circuit T.V. cameras, like dead eyes, unseeing now.

We crossed the border into Northern Ireland.

I'm not sure what we expected. Maybe some terrorist hit men waiting to 'pick off' British tourists as they crossed the border. But all was peaceful today. In fact everything looked remarkably ordinary and British. Even the roads improved. We drove past the shopping centre, and the war memorial where Marie Wilson was killed by an IRA bomb one Remembrance Sunday morning. Past the castle and the museum. I expected Derek to pull into the car park but he didn't stop. I looked at him enquiringly.

"May as well go on to Dungannon," was all he said.

I breathed more easily. When we reached the A4 the traffic was light and Derek put his foot down and the miles sped by. Then, suddenly, we passed into Co. Tyrone. I remembered how, when we were looking through the brochures before booking our holiday, I had intuitively chosen Co. Tyrone.

It was lunch time when we arrived in Dungannon. Derek parked the car just outside the main shopping area and we walked into town. We passed a building where the walls were dorbed with IRA graffiti in white paint and where the Irish flag was flying.

Dungannon proved to be a small, bustling, town like many in England. The only obvious difference were the two armed police officers silently watching the shoppers and I saw that the police station, at the end of the main square, was heavily fortified with steel barricades and barbed wire.

I noticed a war memorial in the centre of the square and we crossed over to look and see if it bore my father's name.

"This is a war memorial to the men of The Royal Inniskilling Fusiliers," observed Derek.

"Bertie was in the Paratroop Regiment."

"The paras were recruited from regular soldiers from other regiments."

"Look here is a Sergeant R. G. White," I said excitedly.

"I wonder what the 'G' stands for?"

"Yes, that is odd," I said thoughtfully. "My grandmother's maiden name was Graham so Bertie was probably known as Robert Graham White."

"'Chalky' White, alias Bertie White, alias Robert White, alias Robert Graham White.

"Quite an elusive character, I agreed.

There was a newsagent opposite the war memorial so we went in to buy some newspapers and hopefully an ordinance survey map of the area. We browsed around the maps that were on display but could not find one that gave the detail we needed.

"We could try the library," I suggested, " I noticed one on the other side of the war memorial."

As Derek stopped to pay for the newspapers I noticed a pile of newspapers called The Dungannon News and Courier. I took one from the pile and handed him the copy.

"Will you buy this for me?"

"Why do you want a local newspaper?"

"I intend to write to the local paper asking if any of their readers remembers my father or any of his friends of relatives," I reminded him.

It was time for lunch so we walked back to the car to eat our sandwiches. Derek spread the map of Ireland out over the dashboard, so that we could study the route to Coalisland. It was the first time I had looked at a map of the area in detail.

"Hey, look at that," I exclaimed, "Coalisland is on the shore of a huge lough."

"Loach Neagh?"

"Yes," I replied thoughtfully, " Did I tell you that I had one of those prophetic dreams when I am almost certain I must have seen Lough Neagh?"

"You have been having a lot of those dreams lately."

"I remember seeing myself sanding on the banks of a vast stretch of water. I knew that this was a place Bertie was very familiar with. A place of significance for him."

We ate our lunch thoughtfully and then walked over the road to the library but the girl behind the desk was unable to help us.

"Why don't you try The Heritage Centre at Donaghmore?" she suggested, "they should be able to help you."

The Heritage Centre proved to be a mine of information and the staff were more than helpful

"I can photocopy part of our map which will give you more detail," said a young assistant. "Then I can look up where the parish boundaries are and mark them on the map."

"That would be wonderful," I said thankfully.

We would have loved to have stayed longer but time was running short, so, armed with the new map, we headed for Coalisland.

It was late afternoon and, following the directions the man had marked on the map we drove in the direction of the parishes of Drumkee and Derrywinner. We pulled off the main road and took the B road that led us away from the housing estate out into open countryside. We saw a signpost pointing the way to 'Bush', which appeared to be in the direction we needed to go.

"I haven't seen any sign post for Drumkee or Derrywinner," I observed.

"No, but according to the map Derrywinner should be on this side of the Bush Road."

It was then that I saw the house on the side of the road.

It was old, deserted now, unlived in, unloved, but there was something very familiar about it. As if I had seen it many, many times before. A landmark my mind was searching for.

"Slow down," I said, "see that house?"

The car slowed.

"I'm not sure how but I know that house...I have seen that house before in my dreams."

"Perhaps your father lived there at some time?"

"It's possible. I have this tingling sensation up my spine...the feeling I get when something significant is going to happen."

Derek drove slowly passed the house. It was a small, white, detached house the windows were broken and slates missing from the roof, it was in dire need of repair. Yet somehow I knew, with complete certainly, that this house had been important to Bertie. Therefore it was important to me.

It was then we noticed the two old men standing by the gates just yards away from the house. I was particularly interested in the older of the two, trying to assess his age. I guessed he was probably near enough to the age my father would have been had he been alive.

I imagined myself getting out of the car and going over to speak to him.

I might say, "excuse me but do you happen to remember my father? He lived here long ago, before the war, his name was Bertie White."

Then, just possibly, the old man might scratch his head and ponder for a while before replying. "Now you come to mention him...I do remember a boy by that name. Someone I went to school with years ago...went away to be a soldier. Killed in the war you know...all very sad."

And, I might hold my breath before asking. "Do you happen to know if he had any relations still living in these parts?"

He would think awhile before replying, "there is a sister lives down the road at number 28. If you knock on her door chances are you'll find her in."

And then...and then!

But I did no such thing on that day. I was too afraid to make myself known because they might reject me.

So, I merely turned to Derek and said, "why don't you turn the car round and ask those two men if this is Derrywinner and how far it is to Drumkee."

He turned the car round and we went back the way we had come, stopping almost opposite the old house. I watched as he approached the men and they turned and spoke to him telling him the way to go. And as I watched them I was aware that something had changed. Whatever it was that had taken possession of my mind that day, had suddenly let go.

I looked across the fields and felt the continuity of the countryside. This is how it had always been, the fields, the trees, the landscape unchanging. If Bertie were here with me now he would recognise it as the same.

Derek opened the car door.

"What did they say?"

"Well, from what I can make out this is Derrywinner, down to the end of the road. Drumkee is up there, turn right."

"I'd like to take some photos but I can't do that just here because they will wonder what I am up to."

"They might think we are English spies," he teased. "I'll drive down to the end of the road and you will get a better view from there."

The men were will still watching us curiously and at the last moment I turned and waved as we drove away. The older of the two lifted his hand in silent salutation.

At the end of the road I took my photographs. The countryside was pleasant but unremarkable with gentle hills, fields and trees, a few cows in a field.

"Do you notice something?" I asked when I had taken enough photographs. "The countryside around here is very similar to where we live in Norfolk. The crops are different but the landscape is much the same."

"Yes, I had noticed. It's similar to the countryside I pass on my way to work driving to Norwich."

Drumkee proved to consist mostly of a few scattered farms with occasional houses, and at the end of the road, a larger house come plant nursery. Outside the nursery was a notice that read 'plants for sale'.

"Lets stop and buy some plants, " I suggested, "I'd like to take some home as a reminder of our visit."

Derek pulled the car onto the driveway and as we got out a youngish woman with dark hair, and wearing casual jeans and jumper, came running out of the house to meet us.

"Hello, can I help you?" she greeted us with a smile.

"We were just passing and I noticed you had some plants for sale?"

"There are some nice fuchsias and geraniums in the greenhouse."

"Great! they should do well in our conservatory."

"Come into the greenhouse and I'll show you what I have."

I followed her into a large polythene greenhouse where every conceivable space was covered with plants.

"It will be hard to choose," I said, "they look nice and healthy."

"Those are weeping fuchsias but if you prefer we have the standard ones on the other side and there are several variety of geraniums."

I chose a selection of fuchsias and geraniums and she found me a cardboard box to put them in.

"I can tell you're not from around these parts," she said with a smile, "are you on your holiday?"

"In a way, we have come over from Norfolk. But my father came from this way," I added.

"We're fairly new here so I don't expect I would remember him."

I don't know why, maybe because she said that she had only recently moved to the area, but I felt I could tell her my reason for coming to Drumkee and Derrywinner.

"My father was killed during the Second World War," I explained. "I never knew him but he was born here in Drumkee and I wanted to see the place where he once lived."

"Have you relations around here?"

"I don't know....it was all so long ago...they are probably all dead by now."

"What was his name?"

"Robert White...but they called him Bertie...he was in the army and was killed in action at the battle of Arnhem.

"There are still Whites living here," she said thoughtfully. They have a farm back there at Derrywinner...and there is a married daughter who lives in a big house."

So the White's still live in this area but how were they related to my father? Probably a younger generation of second or third cousins. Would they have even heard of Bertie White?

"Thank you for that," I said as I paid her for my plants and turned to leave.

Then, with typical Irish generosity she said, "Now let me give you something in return...something to remember Drumkee." She thought for a moment then said, "We have some nice alpine plants round the back, would you like one of those?"

"That's very kind of you," I said following her behind the green house.

"What would you like?"

I spotted some beautiful pots of armeria, "I like those."

"What colour would you like. You have a choice of blue or white?"

"White seems appropriate." We both laughed.

"Here take two," she said placing them in the box before I could refuse.

"Thank you. I shall think of you when I see them growing in my garden."

We shook hands and said good bye. I was so glad that we had stopped to buy some flowers in her nursery. I had discovered my father's relations still lived in the area. In time, God willing, I would return. At that moment I decided I would take one of the pots of white armeria to Arnhem in September and plant them on Bertie's grave. A little part of home.

And so we left Drumkee and drove back to Co. Caven back the way we had come. My mind was peaceful now but I reflected on the significance of the house at Derrywinner. In time I would learn the secret of that place.

CHAPTER TWENTY

That night I slept badly. The nightmares that had haunted me through the years of depression returned. I was alone, rejected, abandoned by those I loved, desperately trying to find my way home. I awoke weeping, though I knew not why.

"What is it?" said Derek, "Why are you crying?"

"I don't know...I was dreaming, terrible dreams, ...I think it was because of yesterday."

"Visiting Bertie's home?"

"Yes. Somehow it was all wrong, it wasn't meant to be like that."

"What do you mean?"

"It should have been a joyful occasion. A triumphant return.....but instead....I went unnoticed, like a thief in the night. I know inside, it wasn't meant to be like that."

"That was how you wanted it. No fuss. No knocking on doors."

"Yes, I know....I know....but it wasn't the way my father wanted me to go home."

"Perhaps, when we come again it will be different."

"Maybe."

And I was comforted.

The force that had driven me so relentlessly over the last two days had deserted me. I felt mentally exhausted, unable to concentrate. We had accomplished all we had set out to achieve. Now I was set free. I could use the remainder of the holiday as I pleased.

We decided to drive to Mullingar, a country town, stopping off at any places that interested us. But when I reached Mullingar the felling of lethargy was so great I could hardly bother to get out of the car. I walked listlessly down the High Street until, sensing my mood, Derek suggested we call it a day.

"Would you like to go back to Multyfarnham," he suggested, "I noticed a Franciscan friary on the way, we could stop off there?"

In my present state of mind the quiet of a friary appealed. The Franciscan friary at Multyfarnham is also a horticultural study center for the friars, and we were happy to discover they had a small garden center that is open to the public.

There were few visitors to be seen as we parked the car. Parts of the friary were out of bounds to tourists but we found a door leading to the chapel of St. Anthony that we might enter.

It was dark inside the chapel in sharp contrast to the brightness of the day and it took a while for our eyes to adjust to the change of light. A kaleidoscope of colour filtered through the stain glass windows dancing on the walls. At the far end of the chapel an impressive statue of the Saint became a focal point for the many novicia candles A multitude of tiny flames merged to create a pool of illumination. The light was inviting, drawing us towards it.

"There is a feeling of timelessness and peace," whispered Derek.

"Yes, it's almost tangible, as if the walls have taken up the countless prayers that have been said here."

We spoke in hushed voices as if afraid to disturb the tranquility of the chapel.

"Would you like to light a candle for your father?"

Lighting a candle was a ritual we observed on such occasions.

"Yes, I will light two, one each for my mother and father."

I chose a red and a blue candle and placed them side by side. Then, taking the lighting taper I set each a blaze. The tiny flames flickered for a moment, uncertain, then, burning more strongly, gave out a steady light.

I sat watching the candles for a time and prayed that the souls of my parents might find peace and enjoy a unity denied to them in their earthly life.

The candles were blazing earnestly now.

I closed my eyes and I was aware of a feeling of peace and calmness, beginning in my mind and spreading outwards, like ripples, until it encompassed my whole being.

Returning to reality I found the mental exhaustion that had clouded my day had evaporated leaving me refreshed, renewed.

Outside, in the startlingly bright world, we walked the rosary way. Life size stone statues marked the stations of the cross. Surprisingly they did not look ghoulish or overdone. The simplicity of the figures blended in perfectly with the naturalness of their surroundings.

We passed a young friar, dressed in jeans and a shirt and wearing a pair of yellow marigold gloves, scrubbing away the mould on a stature of our Lady. An odd combination of the religious and the secular.

***

There was one last place I wanted to visit before we left Ireland, and that was to Lough Neagh. There was none of the compulsion that had driven me to Coalisland before, just a curiosity to see if Lough Nough was the vast stretch of water I has visited in my dream.

As we took the road to Co. Tyrone once again that Thursday any fears we had harbored on our first visit seemed unfounded now. It was a cold, dark day as we arrived at the visitor's center at Lough Neagh. The car park was deserted and there were few people about. I walked down to the water's edge and there before me, as far as the eye could see, lay the lough. A strong wind blew across the surface of the water causing ripples, like waves, that to raced towards me. It was exactly the way I had seen it in my dream. I thought of my father and pictured him in this same place. When had he come, or, with whom? I could only guess. But I felt sure that this was a favourite haunt of his.

Our holiday was almost over; our mission successfully completed. My first task on returning home would be to write to the local newspaper. But, at that moment in time, I had no idea if anyone would answer, or, if so where that would lead me.

CHAPTER TWENTY ONE

When we returned home it was the last week of April, 1995, and I immediately wrote the following letter to the Editor of the Dungannon News and Tyrone Courier.

Dear Sir

I am writing to you in the hope that some of your readers may remember my father, Sergeant Robert (Bertie) White, who was killed in the second World War, at the battle of Arnhem.

I was adopted at birth by my step father and was unaware who my natural father was until after the death of my mother last year. Sadly, any memories my mother had of Bertie died with her.

My husband and I have recently return from Dublin where we went to consult the Irish records for births, marriages and deaths. I discovered that my father was born in Drumkee and at one time lived at Derrywinner. His parents were Elizabeth and Abraham White.

I would love to hear from anyone who remembers my father or my grandparents. Please write to me at the following address....................

Yours sincerely

Susan Arrowsmith.

I had no idea if the newspaper was published daily or weekly, or, how long it would be before my letter appeared in print. Yet, even as I posted the letter, I had the feeling that I had already set the ball rolling. Events would take their course. All I had to do was wait .

It was a strange week that followed our return from Ireland because Monday, 8th May was the 50th anniversary of V.E. day. The end of the war in Europe. The media was full of stories of those final months of the war and the homecoming of those service men and women who returned. My thoughts were constantly of Bertie. Had he survived Arnhem he too would have came home after V.E. day. How different my life would have been then. Would he have taken Mum, Mary and me home to Ireland? Would I have grown up in the countryside around Drumkee and Derrywinner? It would have been a far cry from the bomb damaged streets where we lived in Paddington.

I had a strong feeling that I wanted to celebrate V.E. day this year. Bertie, like many others, had died in an attempt to secure the peace we enjoy today. My children had grown up without the shadow of a world war looming over them as it had for previous generations. In this instance his death had not been in vain.

Derek and I spent the weekend quietly at home. On Monday I attended a special memorial service in the ancient parish church in our village. For once the church was packed to capacity. Many of those who attended were of the war time generation. Among the congregation I noticed several men wearing their military medals, they stood rigidly, faces still, trying to keep control of their emotions. This generation of men rarely cried in public but today I was aware that a man sitting next to me wept openly.

The old church echoed to the sound of the organ and our voices soaring up into the rafters. It occurred to me that this is how it would have been, in this same church 50 years ago.

There was no official wreath laying on the war memorial opposite the church today but I had a posy of red roses that I laid quietly on the memorial when the service had ended.

The message on the card was simple, 'In memory of my father, Sergeant Robert (Bertie) White, who died at Arnhem.

My roses looked vividly red in contrast to the grey stones of the memorial:

Red, for the berets of the men of the Parachute Regiment.

Red, for their blood shed at Arnhem

Red, for the roses that signifies a love that endures.

But today was not just a time for tears. Today we must celebrate the hard won peace. I had baked a special V.E. day cake especially for the occasion. In an attempt to be patriotic I iced the cake blue with the letter V and E in red and with white piping around the edges. The effect was rather startling. After dinner we cut the cake and drunk a toast to Bertie's memory. He occupied my thoughts constantly and he assumed a personality in my mind of the father I hoped he would have been. How would this image alter if I met someone who had known him intimately, a relative or a close friend? Would the image I had of him be sullied in some way. Spoiled. I thought of my letter to the newspaper. How soon would I receive an answer? I felt a moment of apprehension.

I was upstairs in my study when the letter came next day. I heard the rattling of the mail box as the postman pushed the letter through the letterbox and it landed on the mat. A moment later I was retrieving it. The envelope was hand-written, the post mark was Dungannon. Slowly I carried the letter back to my room and slit the envelope, I unfolded the letter, then read the letter twice.

Bush Road

Dungannon

Dear Susan,

I have just read our local paper and your letter to the Editor.

My grandfather was Alexander White and he had a brother Abraham White, and he had a son Robert Graham White (Bertie), who was killed parachuting into Arnhem in 1944. I have a brother Robert White who was in the Royal Artillery stationed in Germany and he has been to visit the grave.

I live in the village of Bush and last week you stopped and asked my father, who was standing by the roadside, where Derrywinner was. This was Bertie's cousin who holds great memories of his cousin as there was just one year difference in their ages. What a pity you didn't go into more details because my father has such great affection for his cousin. If you have ever heard of the bands here in Northern Ireland you should be pleased to hear that the local village band is called the 'Sergeant White memorial flute band'.

We have many photographs of your father and we would be delighted to speak with you and I enclose our telephone number. Robert was from a very close family and you are someone who we have never even guessed about.

Please get in touch, we hope you will not be disappointed.

Doreen Winter (nee White)

Then, still in a state of shock, I picked up the telephone and dialled the number Doreen had given.

CHAPTER TWENTY TWO

It was Daisy that I spoke to on that first day, although at the time I was unsure who I was speaking to.

"Hello is that Doreen?" I heard the tremble in my voice.

"Is that you Susan?" the voice was unmistakably Irish.

"Yes, the postman has just brought your letter....."

"We were trying to get you on the telephone," she told me, "but they said you had an X directory phone number."

"Yes, we had some 'funny' phone calls at one time so we changed to X directory".

"Oh I see," her voice sounded friendlier. "When we couldn't get you on the phone, Doreen, my daughter, wrote to you. She posted it in the main post-box in town and we hoped you might get it by Saturday."

"What a pity, your letter has only come but I phoned right away..." I was fumbling with words not knowing what to say.

Daisy helped we out. "Sandy, he's my husband, who you met on the road was very close to your father. There was only a year between them in age and Bertie lived here in the farmhouse for some time."

My God! I thought Bertie's cousin Sandy was waiting by the side of the road where he and Bertie once lived. So I didn't go home to Derrywinner unnoticed.

"I had no idea if my father still had relations in the area. I only knew that he was born in Drumkee and lived at Derrywinner as a child."

"We hadn't heard about you," she sounded surprised.

"No! I'm sure you haven't because I was adopted by my stepfather and it was only last year, after my mother died, that I heard that Bertie was my father."

I went on to explain, in the best way that I could, all that I knew about my father and how he died at Arnhem. I told her about out trip to Arnhem and visiting my father's grave at Oosterbeek and finally our recent trip to Ireland.

She listened attentively without interrupting me until I had finished my story.

"Well! now we know who you are," she said kindly, "so that's alright."

"And your husband Sandy, he remembers Bertie?" I realised it was a stupid question.

"Yes, they grew up together. Your father came to live here in the farmhouse after your grandfather's house was burned down in a fire."

"Was anyone hurt in the fire?"

"Bertie's younger brother and sister were killed," she told me sadly. along with the housekeeper. Your grandfather, Abraham, went to live with another of his Faloon cousins. Bertie came here."

"Oh no!" I paused trying to keep my voice under control, "How old was Bertie at the time?"

"About 15 I believe...he was the eldest."

"What about my grandmother Elizabeth?"

"She was some sort of invalid and died some time before the fire."

We were both silent for a few moments as I thought over what she had told me about Bertie and his family.

"And then, in the end, Bertie was killed at Arnhem, it must have been terrible for my grandfather to lose his last remaining son so tragically."

"Yes," Daisy said sadly, "When Bertie was killed your grandfather never really took it in. He went into a mental hospital for a time. When he eventually was discharged, years later, he would take a walk each day to the top of the road still waiting for the young lad to come home."

My eyes filled with tears. "How awful so all Bertie's immediate family died?"

"There was a younger sister, Netta, she was only a baby at that time and she was more or less adopted by your grandmother's sister. They moved to England. Never came back even for her father's funeral, or, your Bertie's memorial service," she sighed, "but who could blame her, such tragedies."

"They held a memorial service for my father?" I asked in surprise.

"Yes! Your father is highly thought of round here. There is also a plaque in his memory in the Orange Hall in Bush village and a photograph of him in his army uniform on the wall."

"So my father is a hero in his home town," I said excitedly, "I'd love to see it all."

"You will, when you come again. Then there is his band, they renamed it in his memory after he died."

"Yes, You said in your letter there is the Sergeant White Memorial Band."

"Flute band," she corrected me.

"Of course a flute band!"

Even as she spoke I remembered the sound of the music...and the marching. It was the sound of the flute that I had heard. The sound of the flutes and the marching band. I had a sudden thought. "Did my father ever play in the flute band?"

"Yes, all the White's play in the band. We have some photos somewhere I will send then to you."

"I'd love to have them. I only have one photograph of Bertie when he was in the Paratroop Regiment in the army."

"He joined the Inniskillings before the war it was much later that he went into the Paratroop Regiment."

So Derek had been right.

"What did Bertie do before he joined the army?"

He worked on the farm, his father was a farmer, most of the White's were in those days. Bertie liked to be outdoors. Always had a couple of dogs with him."

I smiled remembering how Derek and I used to picture Bertie White on his allotment with his two dogs. We hadn't been far wrong.

"I've always loved animals and growing things," I added, "I was so different from my brother and sisters. Now I know why."

"Well you are a farmers daughter."

The pieces of the jigsaw were falling effortlessly into place. Generations of my family had farmed the land and reared animals. It was in my genes. I belonged to the land it was part of my very being.

Daisy and I talked for some time exchanging family histories. Daisy told me she had six children and five grandchildren. Her daughter Doreen, who had written the letter to me, lived in what used to be the old farmhouse with her husband Ken. Daisy and Sandy now lived in a new bungalow that had been built next door. Daisy promised to send me some photographs of Bertie and I promised we would visit as soon as we possibly could.

I replaced the telephone receiver and went out into the garden. My mind was desperately trying to come to terms with all that Daisy had told me.

My father, who had lost his mother and then his brother and sister in a fire.

My father, the farmer who loved his dogs and the land.

My father, the war hero, who died at Arnhem.

The pain of realization swept over me and I wept for them all, my grandmother Elizabeth, the children killed in the fire, my grandfather Abraham forever waiting for Bertie to come home from the war....and me....and me......for all the years that might have been. Oh Bertie! My father....my father.

CHAPTER TWENTY THREE

By the time Derek came home for lunch I was reasonably composed.

"Guess what?" I said as he came through the door.

"What?"

"I've had a letter from Dungannon."

"Already?" he sounded shocked.

"Yes, they have been trying to get us on the phone all weekend. I've been talking to Daisy on the telephone."

"Who's Daisy," he asked, "and what did she say?"

I was waiting for this moment. "Well, do you remember the day that we went to Derrywinner, when we stopped and asked an old man standing by the road the way to Drumkee and Derrywinner?" I asked casually.

He thought for a moment, "Yes, we had difficulty understanding each other."

"Well, it seems that he just happened to be Sandy," I paused for effect, "who is probably Bertie's closest living relative. They lived in the farmhouse together until Bertie joined the army. Sandy still farms the same land."

"No!" he looked at me incredulously, as what I had told him sunk in, then he put his face in his hand and was silent for a long time before saying. "That's incredible."

He looked so stricken I had to laugh.

"When you have finished laughing," he said at last, "are you going to show me the letter?"

He read the letter and then I told him all I had learned from Daisy.

"And Daisy is going to send me some photographs," I finished.

"Just like that?"

"Of course, why not?"

"They accepted everything you said....just like that?"

"Well! Daisy did wonder why we hadn't made inquiries when were in the village but when I told her the whole story she was fine."

"That's incredible," he said for a second time, "they seem to be treating you like part of their family."

"I am family."

"I know, but coming out of the blue like that." He picked up the letter and read it once again. "They sound so pleased to hear from you."

"Yes, they do," I said thoughtfully, "all of Bertie's direct family died tragically and now I turn up. The prodigal daughter returns. The phoenix rising out of all that death and destruction...the fire...Arnhem."

"It's like a miracle."

"It is a miracle."

We sat silently for some time, lost in our own thoughts.

"We can't wait until next year," Derek said at last." We will have to go back to Ireland this year."

"I was thinking the same thing," I replied. "Maybe we can go again in the autumn after our visit to Oosterbeek."

But we did not have to wait that long.

It was Derek who took the next call from my cousin Doreen the following Thursday evening, while I was working at the nursing home. He phoned later to tell me about it.

"I've just had a long conversation with your cousin Doreen."

"Have you?" I said with some surprise. "What did she say?"

"I'll tell you the whole story tomorrow, but to cut a long story short, they have invited us to go and stay with them in July."

"Really?"

"Yes, really, she says the couldn't wait until next year to meet you."

"Did you tell her we felt the same?"

"Seems there are lots of relations and friends of your father who want to meet you."

"Great," I said excitedly, "I will find out all I want to know about Bertie. Doreen sounds like a nice person."

"She is, very, I'm sure you will get on well with her. She sounds as if she is on your wave length."

"How do you mean?"

"Well, when I told her about all the coincidences, all the strange things that have happened, she said the spirits are guiding you home."

I smiled and, of course, Doreen was right, the spirits were guiding me home.

CHAPTER TWENTY FOUR

It was arranged. We were to sail from Stranraer to Larne, in Northern Ireland, on the 8th July. We would spend a week with Doreen and Ken at the farm house where Bertie lived before he joined the army. I had several telephone conversation with Doreen and it never ceased to amaze me that I was speaking to someone related to my father who was actually living in the house he had once called home.

Events had moved fast. From knowing virtually nothing about my father, through my conversations with Daisy and Doreen, I was building up a picture of his life which, hopefully would be enhanced during the coming visit.

Bertie, it seems, was the eldest of four children; the others being Frederick, Mary and Netta, the youngest who was virtually adopted by her aunt after my grandmother's early death. At the time of the fire in 1929 Bertie was 15 years of age. The family were living in a large, three storey, house in the village of Moy. The fire, it was rumoured, was started deliberately, although no one was ever charged with the crime. It was around midnight when the fire broke out, sweeping through the large rooms of the old house with devastating speed. Bertie and his father jumped for their lives from an upstairs window. The housekeeper and the two younger children died in the fire.

After the house was burned down Bertie went to live with his White cousins on the farm at Derrywinner. Grandfather Abraham stayed, a few miles away, with his sister who had married one of the Faloons, and her family.

Bertie and his cousin Sandy grew very close during this period of their lives. The boys worked on the farm, still famous for the 'White's' early potatoes, and the dairy farm. In their spare time the boys, like many other youngsters, played in the village flute band and, later, were to become members of the Orange Order. When they were not occupied with farm work the two boys loved to spend days out hunting in the countryside with their dogs. Sandy told me later, when I had got to know him, that sometimes they disappeared and spent the whole day fishing at Loche Neagh. No wonder I had been drawn to that place.

When Bertie was 16 he and a friend made a spur of the moment decision that was to change his life for ever. They signed up to join the Royal Inniskilling Fusiliers. They lied about their age and this is why Bertie's grave at Oosterbeek states that he was aged 32 when he was killed. His friend was turned down due to a medical condition Bertie was left on his own now to face the music. Afraid to go home and face his father with what he had done he spent the night camping out in the barn. After, Bertie joined his regiment, Sandy remained at the farm in Derrywinner. Later, Sandy married his wife Daisy and with their children continued to live in the same farmhouse.

The week before we were due to leave for Ireland I went into hospital for a simple surgical procedure which would be carried out under general anesthetic. I was to be admitted on the morning of the operation, and, if all went well I would be allowed home that evening. On my return from the operating theatre, I have a hazy recollection of being lifted from the trolley into my hospital bed where I drifted in and out of consciousness.

At some point I must fallen asleep and I dreamed that I was standing outside of a house that appeared familiar to me. The house was detached and on its own well away from any other houses. From the style of the house I guessed it was a probably a substantial, detached, Georgian , or early Victorian house, fronted with stone and with a slate tiled roof. I walked up to the solid, wooden front door but even as I did so I has the feeling that this door was only opened on special occasion. Instead I made my way round the house to the back door. This door was open and I walked through into a large room with a welcoming feel, obviously the kitchen was the hub of the house. I noticed a kettle boiled merrily on an enormous black cooking range. A white pine top table, held center space surrounded by an assortment of chairs and benches, whilst an old fashion dresser containing crockery stood against a wall. There were two doors leading from the kitchen, though one I could see a scullery area, the other door led into the hall. From here I noticed that there were two other rooms downstairs. I glanced into the larger of the two rooms and this seemed to be the 'posh' living room. Some of the furniture was covered as if the room were seldom used and it had a cold, uninviting feel. I did not stay long. Instead I went into the smaller room which was situated next to the front door. This room felt warm and comfortable and was obviously well used. It was filled with an assortment of furniture and useful farm paraphernalia. A slight smell of tobacco smoke lingered in the air. I sat in a high backed chair and knew this was where Bertie had sat many times.

Eventually I decided to explore upstairs and returning to the hall I saw a wooden staircase leading to the floor above. The stairs were narrow and covered with a faded carpet and the curved hand rail looked well used. On the second floor I passed a door, slightly ajar, I peeped inside and saw an old fashioned bathroom that smelt faintly of lavender, with a huge white bath and a toilet with an overhead water system and chain.

Finally I entered what was a large bedroom with widows on two sides of the room. There were two double beds, that struck me as being particularly high, that took up most of the remaining space. I went to each window in turn and from the first window I could see the view from the front of the house and a well trodden path that led to the road. The window on the far side of the room looked out on to farm land and I could make out farm buildings and a large barn. I knew there were other rooms but this was as much of the house that I was to see on that occasion, or any other, for the next thing I remember was the nurse waking me with a cup of tea.

Derek collected me from the hospital that evening. I had expected to suffer some discomfort for a couple of days but by Monday I was in severe pain and feeling extremely ill. A visit to the doctor confirmed I was suffering from a uterine infection. The doctor order me to go home to bed, with the improviso that if I did not improve quickly, I would be readmitted to hospital. Only four days until we were due to leave for Ireland and things were looking pretty bleak. Derek and I made a pact that unless I showed sign of improvement by Thursday evening the trip would have to be postponed.

Tuesday and Wednesday passed in a blur. I slept a great deal and when I did dream it was always the same dream of the house. After a while I became bored with the dream and hoped the next time it would be different, or I might see more of the house, but it never changed.

Thursday came and thankfully I had was considerably better. That evening I was able to phone Daisy and make the final arrangement for meeting us on our arrival.

CHAPTER TWENTY FIVE

Saturday, 8th July, dawned bright and sunny. We left home very early in the morning as we had calculated the journey to Stranraer would take at least eight house, without allowing for possible delays. Our journey would take us through the heart of England, via the A1, the south to Scotland and Stranraer. For the first couple of hours we made good progress but by mid-morning we were delayed by road works and the traffic built up considerably. We were glad we had allowed plenty of time.

It was 5pm when we eventually arrived, tired and hungry, at the port. From the number of cars queuing for the ferry, it was obviously going to be far more crowded than when we sailed in April. Everyone, it seemed, wanted to be home for the Orange Parade holiday. Eventually the crew began loading the cars and at last, we found ourselves on board.

"Let's go and have something to eat before the restaurant gets too crowded," I suggested.

We found the restaurant and had a leisurely meal. A couple of hours to go and we would be landing in Larne, a few miles from Belfast. Doreen had arranged to meet us on a slip road off the motorway and then to escort us the remainder of the way to their home at Derrywinner.

By the time we had finished our meal the ship was very crowded. Throngs of peoples occupied the bars and entertainment areas. Everywhere we saw noisy, excited children, demanding attention. It seemed impossible to find somewhere where we could relax quietly and recuperate after our long journey. Eventually, we made our way up to the sun deck. Few people had penetrated this far. It was getting late but it remained reasonably warm and so we found a seat where hopefully we could relax and be undisturbed for the remained of the voyage.

I closed my eyes and soon the gentle throbbing of the ships engines combined with the rhythmic rolling of the ship, lulled me into a drowsy half sleep. My head fell sideways and although the seat next to me was empty, it was as if my head fell onto someone's shoulder. I was aware of a roughness of cloth next to my cheek and the slight smell of a cigarette. It was as if I were a small child and someone was holding me close, protecting me.

Somewhere in the back of my mind a voice I recognized said "go to sleep Susie darling and we'll soon be home. We'll soon be home."

Sinking deeper into sleep I felt myself cocooned in a feeling of love and security, while all the while a soft Irish voice was softly singing half remembered songs from long, long ago.

Suddenly, a door near me closed with a slam. I was jolted into instant awareness. Turning to my companion I meant to say, "Daddy, are we home yet?"

When in the same split second, realization came, like a dagger through my heart, that I was 52 years of age, and I must make the journey home on my own.

CHAPTER TWENTY SIX

Doreen's grey Citron pulled into the drive ahead of us. It was past 11pm and dark now but I had been surprised how light the sky had remained on the drive from Larne.

Doreen and Daisy had met us on the last leg of our journey on a junction off the motorway.

"Welcome to Ireland Susan," said Daisy warmly from the passenger seat of Doreen's car.

And it was their warmth that I noticed first about them. That and their cornflower blue eyes. Nearly all the Whites' have this particular colour eyes. And so has my son David. Something that always puzzled me in the past as I have dark eyes and Derek's are a different shade entirely. Now the mystery was solved David had inherited his grandfather's eyes.

We followed Doreen's car as she pulled up outside the house. It was then that I felt a sense of shock. The house bore no resemblance at all to the house in my dream. In life it was larger, more prestigious with an imposing porch and upstairs bay windows. How could I have been so totally wrong?

Even so, as I climbed out of the car I was ready to make my way to the back door, as I had so often in my dreams. Before I could do so, however, the front door was opened and Ken, Doreen's husband, was there to welcome us with the two dogs Shamus, a black labrador and Trudy a small, white crossbred bitch.

Ken ushered us into a small room while Doreen disappeared to make us a much needed cup of tea. I sat in an armchair near to the door and as I did so I realised I had sat in this room before. It had changed drastically. This was the small room of my dream that had been a favourite of Bertie's.

We sat up talking into the early hours of the morning. Derek and I had reached the point of being overtired and past sleep. Gradually we learned something of Ken and Doreen's life and things became clearer. Doreen had lived for many years in England where she had met and married Ken. It was only in recent years that they had returned to live in Ireland. At that time the farmhouse had not been lived in for many years and was in urgent need of repair. Sandy and Daisy lived in a bungalow they had built nearby. Doreen and Ken decided drastic measures where called for and the original house was reduced to a mere shell and almost entirely rebuilt. An extra wing was added as was the front section of the house. Now my dream made sense. I had seen the house how Bertie remembered it over 50 years ago.

When Doreen showed us around I discovered the rooms, although transformed beyond recognition remained in the same position as I visualized them. The 'posh' room was now an extremely smart sitting room; whilst the kitchen was fitted with pine units and a green solid fuel aga cooker. Even the stairs were wider. What interested me was when Doreen showed us to our room. The bedroom had windows on opposite sides of the room and were just as I had seen them in my dreams.

I slept fitfully that night; I was full of a restless energy that would not let me sleep. Once I awoke, and seeing the windows of either side of the room thought I was back in my dream. Several times during the night I was up, prowling the landing, on my way to the bathroom at the end of the corridor. The landing window looked down over what was the farm yard and old farm buildings. The dawn broke and I was able to see clearly the old brick buildings and the new barn where Ken now kept his show budgerigars. The old barn is run down and seldom used nowadays but in my mind's eye I could see two boys down there getting in the cows and loading the milk wagon ready for the daily round.

At length my watch showed 8am and I judged it a decent hour to slip down to the kitchen to make a cup of tea. Oddly enough I never felt a stranger in that house. It was as if I were returning to a much loved home after many, many years away. The house may have changed beyond recognition but in essence it felt the same.

SUSAN OUTSIDE THE WHITE'S FARMHOUSE IN DERRYWINNER

There was something I had wanted to do on that first morning at Derrywinner, and that was to attend the morning service in the parish church where my grandparent's were buried. It was my way of acknowledging that some kindly deity, far greater than my own psychic power, had aided me on my quest. It was hard to believe that just over a year ago all I had known about my father was the name 'Bertie White', who had once been a paratrooper and now, by some miracle, I was staying in his family home.

However, it was with some trepidation that I greeted Doreen with the news that I was off to attend a service in the parish church. If she was surprised she did not show it. She wasn't sure of the times but seemed to think the service was either at 10 or 11 am. Derek and I decided to drive into the village of Moy in time for 10am. If we were early we could spend the time sight seeing.

Moy proved to be a pleasant large country village with the usual collection of shops and the village church at its center There were flowers everywhere. The local people take great pride in the village and the council had filled any open space with flower beds and hanging baskets. There was a well kept war memorial, surrounded with flower beds, opposite the church. I found my father's name, White R G, inscribed on the stone with the names of all those how had lost their lives in the great wars.

Even on a Sunday morning there were a number of people about. We found the church easily enough and from the notice board read the service would not be until 11 am.

"What would you like to do for an hour," asked Derek.

"I noticed there is a grave yard at the back of the church. Let's see if we can find my grandparent's grave."

We opened the gate and made for a section of the churchyard where the graves stones looked older than the rest.

"Let's start over there," I suggested, "grandmother Elizabeth died over 60 years ago."

But we were out of luck that morning. We examined each head stone but found none bearing my grandparent's names.

"They could be in an unmarked grave," suggested Derek.

"That's possible," I sighed, "we shall have to ask Sandy and Daisy and try again another day."

Back in the street a small crowd was gathering.

"What's going on?" I asked.

"Doreen said there might be an Orange march."

"We may as well wait and see," I replied, "the vicar is standing outside the church so they can't start without him."

A few minutes later we heard the sound of the band heralding the Orange men's parade. Then came the Orange men themselves. The walked in solemn procession. All wore the collars and armlets of their Orange order and many of the older men wore bowler hats. We expected the crowd of on onlookers to cheer but the procession passed silently.

"They're going into the church," I observed, "that's what the vicar waiting for." What are you going to do?" asked Derek. "The church will be packed out with that lot and you won't get in."

"I'm going after them," I said bravely, "you wait for me in the car."

I gave them a few minutes to get well ahead then followed them into the church.

Inside, the church was packed to overflowing.

"There's room upstairs," a church warden told me kindly and pointed to where a circular staircase lead to a balcony above. From there I had a birds eye view of the congregation. I felt slightly intimidated looking down on the sea of men of the Orange Order below. But it was too late to retreat because any route of access was now closed to me until the service was over.

The service began and the band played loudly whilst the congregation sung the hymns lustily. It was then time for the vicar to give his long sermon. I thought wistfully of home and Father John's gentle, comforting sermons.

"Is he ever going to stop?" I heard a girl behind me whisper to her companion.

It seemed not. However, even the most fervent of clergymen has to finish sometime and eventually I was able to follow the Orange Order out of the church.

"I was getting worried about you," said Derek, "was it a good service?"

"Say it was an experience; through not quite what I had in mind."

The band was striking up once more and we watched the Orange men march away.

"Bertie belonged to the Orange Order," I remembered, "he probably marched here in much the same way."

As we found our way back to the car I had a feeling of disappointment. The morning hadn't lived up to my expectations. I hadn't found my grandparents' grave and the service was far from the uplifting experience I had hoped for. But we had seen our first Orange parade. Now it was time to go home and meet my father's family.

We drove back down the Bush Road to Derrywinner. The farm house was well back from the road and I was looking for a landmark I recognized.

"Why there's that old house," I exclaimed in surprise, "I didn't notice it in the dark last night."

"We must be nearly there then," said Derek, "keep an eye open for the drive."

He approached the house slowly and found the drive a few yard from it. In fact, the house was the landmark, visible from the road and from the farm house.

"Do you realise that when we stopped by the house the first time we came to Derrywinner, we were virtually stopping outside my father's home.

"And Sandy just happened to be there to see us," said Derek.

"I'm like a homing pigeon who instinctively knew its way

home."

"Or, the spirits might have had a hand in it."

"Yes," I agreed, "the spirits had a hand in it."

DAISY, KEN, DOREEN, DEREK - AT THE WHITE'S
BUNGALOW

CHAPTER TWENTY SEVEN

Sunday afternoon, the moment I had been waiting for, it was time to meet my father's family. Doreen and Ken walked with us the short distance from the farm house to the bungalow where Sandy and Daisy now lived. Doreen had already warned me not to expect too much from Sandy on our first meeting.

"He's a quiet man, takes him time to get to know you, but he will tell you all you want to know in his own time."

The bungalow already seemed full of people, mainly Daisy and Sandy's children and grandchildren. I found Sandy sitting in his favourite armchair, with his pipe, and his pet budgerigar on a table next to him. Doreen introduced us and I kissed him on the cheek and told him how happy we were to be with them. He was a tall man, his hair was white now, but still thick and curly, and he had the blue eyes, characteristic of the White's. I knew he was near enough in age to my father, so he would now be in his 80th year, yet he could easily have passed for 10 years younger.

Daisy introduced us to her son Robert, the same name as my father, who like his namesake, was also a soldier Some years earlier, when he was based in Germany, Robert had visited my father's grave at Oosterbeek. He, more than any of us, understood the catastrophe of that ill fated mission.

But it was dear aunt Meme, Sandy's sister, who went straight to my heart.

"Now come and sit with me," she said patting a place on the settee beside her, "then we can have a nice chat."

"You remember my father?"

"Very well dear, we all lived together at the big house. When mother died it was left to us girls to look after them all."

"So you were like a sister to him?"

"We were all very close. He came to us after that terrible fire," she pressed my hand, "a terrible tragedy."

"Daisy said he was about 15 at the time of the fire?"

"Yes and Mary, Bertie's sister, was younger."

"What did Bertie do after the fire?"

"Bertie and his father spent the night of the fire in the workhouse. Then the family rallied round and Bertie came to live here to Derrywinner."

"Sandy was very fond of your father and they were up to a few tricks up there, I can tell you."

"When did he join the army?"

"Let me see,....he was still very young."

"Was it something he talked about doing?"

"Not that I know of but boys will be boys. Two older boys from the village talked him and his mate into it. They all went off to Dungannon and signed up for the Inniskillings.

"Were you surprised?"

"In a way," she patted my arm again, "but there was nothing here for him here dear."

"Was he happy in the army?"

"Seemed to be, travelled all over the world, spent a long time in Singapore."

"Then he joined the Paratroop Regiment?"

"Yes, but that was later during the war."

"Did he come home often?"

"At first, but then he was stationed at Dungannon, but later he came home whenever he got leave."

"Do you remember the last time he came home?"

"I'll always remember those days dear," I could see her going back in time. "It was just before D Day. He was telling us all that the next time he came home he would be coming home from France," she paused and her voice dropped, "the day before he was due to leave, he said, Meme, I've got this feeling I'll never come home again and he wept on my shoulder....."

"So my father had a premonition he would not come home again?"

"Yes," she sighed, "I think he probably did."

But it was not a day to be sad so we set aside the painful memories. Daisy had one of the boys go up to the loft and bring down two old photograph albums that had belonged to my father.

"They were sent home with his possession after he died," she explained.

As Derek and I looked through the album we noticed that many of the more personal photographs were missing, obviously given to members of the family over the years. In fact, Daisy had sent me some of the photos in her first letter. Those that remained were meticulously stuck in the albums with those 'corners' we used years ago. There were lots of photos of army friends and views of places he visited. Several were of pretty, oriental girls he probably met whilst out East. The second album contained many postcards, he obviously had a keen interest in the cinema, as there were lots of cards of film stars, particularly Shirley Temple and Greta Garbo.

As we came to the end of the albums another visitor arrived. It was Albert Falloon, someone I was anxious to meet. The Falloons were cousins of my father, and I remembered that it was my grandfather's sister, Mary Jane Falloon, whose family had given grandfather a home in the last tragic years of his life.

Albert Falloon looked to be in his forties. He was fairly tall with sandy red hair and blue eyes, but most of all I remember his mad sense of humour, he found fun in everything. Later I was to learn it was not always so. At one time, following a terrible accident, his life had hung in the balance.

He came over to greet me the moment he entered the room.

"I've got you some photographs," he told me as he handed me a envelope. He watched eagerly as I took them out and looked at them. There were two of my father. One was a formal army photograph, taken in uniform, in which he looks very young and somehow vulnerable. The other was taken some years later, in civilian dress, in which he is wearing a suit. It shows a handsome, serious looking, young man with dark curly hair and light colored eyes. When I look at these photographs today I am aware of sense a of sadness about him as if, even then, he guessed his fate. The last photograph was one of an elderly man, out in a field, helping with the harvest.

"My grandfather?" I asked eagerly.

"Yes, I had it enlarged. It looks just like him."

I was deeply moved and I stood up and kissed him on the cheek.

"Do you like them," he replied, and I could see that he was pleased.

"Yes, thank you so much, they are wonderful."

I was to meet Albert several times during my stay at Derrywinner and found I had much to be grateful to him for. It was he, more than anyone else, who had kept the Sergeant White Memorial Band going. Doreen told me that at one time almost all the members of the band were Whites or Falloons. Albert recruited young people from the neighborhood, seeing it also as a way of keeping them off the streets and so helping to keep them out of trouble. I am sure my father would approve whole heartedly.

CHAPTER TWENTY EIGHT

Orange day was not until Wednesday so Derek and I had two days to fill as we pleased. For Doreen and Ken it was work as usual. So it was, that on Monday morning, we found we had the house to ourselves. We planned to drive into Enniskillen and visit the castle and regimental museum.

Before we left I decided to take the opportunity to go for a walk on my own. I let myself out by the back door and strolled down to the field where the pickers were gathering the early potatoes. A pile of bikes, belonging to the pickers, lay at the entrance of the field. I followed the path through the field and in the distance I could see Sandy walking ahead of me. His tall, bent figure, walked doggedly with the aid of a stick, to where the pickers were stacking the sacks onto the lorry. He stopped to talk to a man and I could see them earnestly examining the potatoes. There was a timeless quality about the scene. So it must always have been at Derrywinner. I pictured Bertie and Sandy harvesting the White's early potatoes. Now a new generation of pickers had taken their place. Did Sandy remember those days or had the years blurred in his memory, each potato season fading into the last?

I continued my walk passing the barn where the cows and their calves were housed. They looked at me with their gentle eyes, watching, unconcerned, as I opened the gate into the field where they were allowed to graze. The grass was lush and green, a sky lark sung high in the sky above me as I walked to the end of the field. From here I could see the countryside for miles around. And as I walked it was as if someone walked with me. If I were to glance round quickly I would see them. There was a sense of excitement in the air. And, you may think me fanciful, but I had this curious feeling that a couple of excited dogs were running around my heels. This feeling became so intense that, at times, I felt the need to quiet them. Then realised there was nothing to be seen. Ghosts of the past perhaps?

That evening Sandy and Daisy joined us at the farmhouse for dinner? We sat round the table in the kitchen as the family had always done in the past. Hopefully, would continue to do so in the years to come. There was a feeling of continuity, of security, knowing that he routine of daily life remained the same.

I imagined my father coming home unexpectedly on leave. Who ever happened to be at home would automatically have laid an extra place at the table. However far away from home he happened to be he could rely on the continuity of life at Derrywinner.

Later, that same evening, after the dinner things were cleared away, we walked with the dogs to the gate that overlooked the field where the cows grazed. Sandy, in more talkative mood, told me how he and Bertie loved to go into this field to hunt for rabbits. How Bertie used to laugh when the excited dogs were set free to run wild. From then on that field became Bertie's field to me.

DEREK WITH SHAMUS IN BERTIE'S FIELD AT DERRYWINNER

CHAPTER TWENTY NINE

Wednesday, 12th July, the day of the Orange men's marches. It was a tradition in Bush to see the marchers off from the Orange Hall in the village. But I was eager to see the Orange Hall for another reason. It was here, shortly after the war ended, that the local people held a memorial service for my father in which a memorial plaques was dedicated to his memory.

A small crowd was already gathering when we arrived with Doreen. It had been raining overnight and the sky was grey and overcast but the forecast was for a bright day. Outside the hall the members of the band, wearing their smart red and blue military style uniforms, were preoccupied with last minute preparations. As we approached Albert Falloon appeared from inside the hall and immediately ushered me in.

He left me then, recognizing it was a moment I needed to be on my own.

The plaque was situated on a wall in the center of the room. Above it hung a large black and white photograph of my father in his army uniform. It must have been taken when he was in his mid-twenties. It shows a serious young man, wide eyed, looking into the distance. Seeing the destiny that awaited?

His cap badge from the Inniskilling Fusiliers had been embedded in the stone plaque which was inscribed with the words.

TO THE MEMORY OF

SERGEANT ROBERT G. WHITE

KILLED IN ACTION AT ARNHEM SEP. 1944

'HE DIED THAT WE MIGHT LIVE'

I could easily have wept, but the daughter of a war hero is not expected to cry on such occasions.

Outside in the road the band and members of the Orange Order were forming up ready to leave. I wanted to get some photographs so I hurriedly joined Doreen outside. They made a brave sight in their brightly colored uniforms and peaked caps and I felt enormously proud for my father. There were three drummers in the lead, followed by the large bass drum, around which were the words 'Sergeant White's Memorial Band'. I remembered how, only a few months ago, I had been afraid that my father was forgotten. Only to discover that, 50 years after his death, he is a legend in his home town. An honour few of us can aspire to.

They were ready to leave. The drummers beat out the rhythm and the flute players, picking up the tune, began to play. I remembered the sound well. I had heard it before in my dream.

But what was the significance of that dream? Daisy had told me Bertie had played in the band when he was young. Is this how he wanted me to remember him?

I watched the band march away until the sound was lost to me. We then drove back to the farm where Sandy and Daisy were preparing to drive to Cough where we would see the full Orange Parade. Doreen and Ken, having seen it many times in the past, had decided to stay at home.

Daisy drove the car round the back way to Cough and so avoiding the congested main road. She drove speedily down the narrow, winding roads, emerging triumphantly on to the main road just a few hundred yards from the field which was being used as a temporary car park. The traffic was almost at a standstill at this point. A couple of police officers directing the traffic to the allotted parking areas. The top field was already packed to capacity so we had to park further down and walk up the hill to the field where the marchers would end their parade.

There was a holiday atmosphere on the field. Stalls selling food, ice cream, toys and souvenirs were all doing a steady trade. A raised platform had been erected in a prominent position from where the speeches would be made later in the day. We had brought our own fold up chairs from the car and these we now set up in a favorable position near to one of the stalls serving food. Daisy always patronized this particular stall as she said they gave good value for money.

"Are you ready for a sandwich and a cup of tea?" she asked once we were settled.

"Yes please."

"Ham or cheese?"

Derek and I looked at each other, "cheese please," we echoed in unison.

"Let me give you a hand I offered."

I joined Daisy in the queue at the stall. It was obviously one of the more popular ones and was doing a brisk turnover. There was nothing fancy about the food, just sandwiches, cakes and drinks, but it was well prepared and pre-packed.

"Two cheese and two ham," called Daisy when it was our turn,

"We get a sandwich, a bun and a cup of tea for £1.50." she informed me.

No wonder this stall was so popular. A lady handed we a bag containing our sandwiches and buns whilst another lady was pouring cups of tea into disposable cups. I had £5 in my hand ready to offer her.

"Put that money away," said Daisy, catching sight of the offending £5 note, "I'm going to pay for us all." She looked mortally offended so I hastily thrust my £5 in my pocket. There is a certain unwritten code of Irish hospitality that only a fool would break.

More and more people arrived. Daisy and Sandy seemed to know them all. We spotted aunt Meme, looking slightly harassed because she had been stuck in the traffic for ages. Robert and his wife with their three children came to join us. The girls wanted burgers and chips so disappeared in the direction of two rival fast food vans.

"Will this be your first Orange Parade," Robert asked.

"Yes, we've nothing like it in England."

"You will enjoy it the first time," he assured us, "after the third time you will get a bit bored and every year after that you wonder what you are doing here, but you still come."

There was some movement at the gate at the far end of the field and we could hear the distant sounds of the bands. The marchers would parade through this gate before finally dispersing at the other end of the field. The first band came into sight leading in their Orange Lodge. I waited, camera poised to get some good shots. I took pictures of all the leading bands before it dawned on me that I would soon run out of film. There were different bands, brass bands, pipe bands, flute bands, steel bands and every combination, all with their own distinctive uniforms. Following each band came the Orange men carrying the banner of their Lodge. Our band came into sight half way through.

"That looks like our band," I said excitedly, "I must get some good pictures.

I pushed myself in front of the crowd and managed to get them clearly in the viewfinder.

"Why don't you come and sit down," called Daisy, "there are still plenty more to see."

The family, having prudently placed their chairs in an advantageous position, were sitting watching the marchers in comfort. Half an hour later I had to admit my feet were hurting and sank thankfully into a chair offered by one of the girls.

"Are you getting band overload?" asked Robert.

"Not yet," I laughed, "but I have to admit I never thought there would be so many."

"This is a short parade, some are twice as long," he assured me.

I caught sight of the Bush band coming round for a second time.

"Don't tell me they go round twice.

Daisy laughed "No, you don't have to worry Susan, some Orange Lodges haven't their own bands so they pay a band to lead them in.

Finally, after over two hours, the march came to an end. I had seen my first Orange day march.

"We don't stay for the speeches," Daisy informed us so we packed up the chairs and made our way back to the field where the car was parked.

"How did you enjoy your first Orange day," asked Doreen when we arrived home.

"It was amazing. I can see now why it's so much part of life."

"It was very important to your daddy, that's why I wanted you to come for the marching season. He played in the band himself and was a member of the Bush Orange Lodge."

"Yes, and I'm glad I was able to come and see for myself," I told her gratefully.

We sat in the comfortable farm house kitchen drinking our tea and talking about our lives. I listened to Doreen telling me about her childhood here on the farm and I though back to my childhood in Paddington. It seemed light years away from the life Doreen was describing. How curious to think if my daddy had lived it would have been my life also.

"Would you care to see the Bush boys march home?" she asked at length.

"Another Bush tradition?" I laughed.

"Oh, you don't have to if you've had enough marching for one day," she hastily assured me.

"I wouldn't miss it for the world."

We joined the familiar gathering at Bush cross roads. There were more people than there were this morning. I could see mothers with young children excitedly waiting to wave the marchers home. I noticed how many of the children had the

White's blue eyes.

"Most of these people are third or fourth cousins to you," Doreen said as if reading my mind.

We stood at the corner of the road waiting for the marchers to appear over the brow of the hill.

"They won't be long now," said Doreen, "they park their coach then march the remainder of the way home."

I waited. I could not yet see them but, carried on the still air, I thought I heard the sound of a flute, or, was it my imagination. I stained my ears,....listening,..........the sound was louder now. I could make out the tune they were playing. I could hear the marching of many feet They were coming....nearer...nearer.

I was reliving my dream but this time as the Sergeant White Memorial Band came marching over the brow of the hill. I was there to meet them.

I knew then, as I stood watching my father's band marching home, that this was how he wanted to be remembered. He didn't want me to dwell on his death at Arnhem but rather to remember his life here at Derrywinner. As those who loved him still did by keeping his memory alive through the Sergeant White Memorial Band.

THE SERGEANT WHITE MEMORIAL BAND

CHAPTER THIRTY

The march was over and we left them at the village hall to their celebration meal. Derek and I were going to join them later after having dinner with my family at the farmhouse. We would then have the opportunity of meeting some of the local people who remembered Bertie.

Dinner was a leisurely affair with much cheerful discussion about the days Orange march and it was already becoming dusk when we went back of Bush village hall. Inside the tables remained laid up in a horseshoe fashion, with the top table at the far end of the hall and two rows of table running the length of the walls.

Sitting at the top table was an elderly lady, she was small and frail, like a little bird but she noticed me immediately and her eyes lit up and she smiled warmly as I entered the hall as if she had been waiting for me to arrive. I returned her smile instinctively and I realised, even without being introduced, that she was Florrie Meenagh, a dear friend of Bertie's, who had seen him off at the railway station at the end of his last leave. Doreen lead me over to be introduced.

"Susan this is Florrie Meenagh, an old friend of your father's," said Doreen.

"Hello Florrie, I've wanted so much to meet you," I said as I took her hand."

"Your really are Bertie's daughter?" her eyes scanned my face for some sign of recognition.

"Yes, I am Bertie's daughter, Susan."

She looked at me with a look of wonder in her eyes. Who did

she see? A ghost from her past?

"They tell me you were at school with Bertie?"

"Yes, we were always friends right from when we were children. We grew up together you see," she smiled and her eyes looked past me as she remembered. "Then later, after he joined the army, we always met up whenever he came home on leave."

It was noisy in the hall and I had to bend closer to catch her words.

"They told me you saw him off on his last leave?"

"Yes," she sighed, "that last leave. He came home as he always did turning up unexpectedly, out of the blue but I was always so happy to see him ." She grew more serious. "Then, on that final day, I went with him to see him off at the station, " her eyes misted over. "We kissed goodbye and then he was gone. I never saw him again."

"His death must have come as a terrible shock?"

"I couldn't believe it when they told me he was dead. " unshed tears came into her eyes. "I saw him off at the station just the same as usual and he said he was going back to camp that day....." her words faltered. "We didn't know anything about him going to Arnhem until we heard it on the news." She was silent for a time and I waited patiently for her to continue. "Then, after the war, we held a memorial service for him right here in this hall. That was when they put the plaque up in his memory." She looked in the direction of the photograph on the wall, "I cried my eyes out all the way through the service, she smiled a watery smile, "through all thy hymns and reading."

"You never forgot him?"

"Never, her voice lowered, "I have paid for a wreath to be laid at the war memorial in Moy every years since the war ended."

I felt a lump in my throat because I knew without a shadow of doubt that Florrie Meenagh had truly cared for Bertie, and still did after all these years.

"Thank you," I whispered and lent over and kissed her on the cheek.

We held hands, without speaking, two women from different worlds bound by the love we shared for my father. We continued to talk for some time with Florrie telling me stories about when she and Bertie were children. I could see that she was growing tired and at length her son returned and said it was time for her to go.

"I will see you when I come again," I promised.

I watched her leave and thought how different Bertie's life would have been if he had stayed at home and married Florrie Meenagh.

The hall was crowded now and I remained seated at the top table with Derek and Doreen. People looked at me curiously and eventually one of the men that I recognized from the Orange parade came over to speak to me.

"Is it true that you are Sergeant White's daughter?" he asked cautiously.

"Yes, it's true," I smiled.

His face broke into a broad smile and he held out his hand and shook mine furiously. "My, it's an honour to meet you," he said letting go of my hand. "We read about you in the paper...amazing....."

I laughed, "It was just as much as a surprise to me to discover so many of Bertie's relatives and friends still living here. And, of course, the wonderful Memorial Band."

"Your father is still well respected hereabouts, always has been," he said seriously, "and if you are his daughter you are more than welcome," he finished warmly.

I felt the tears at the back of my eyes. It certainly was turning into an emotional evening.

"Thank you, I am so happy to be here with you all," I managed at last.

He stayed for a while talking about my father and then another of the Orange men came to join us. Again I was introduced and shook hands.

"Let me get you a drink," said the second after the introductions.

He went away to fetch me a rum and blackcurrant, the only drink I could think of to ask for. Before he came back there were several other men waiting to be introduced to me. I looked up at my father's photograph on the wall and he appeared to be looking straight at me. 'This is your moment Father, I thought, I hope you are feeling proud?' But even as the thought entered my mind the voice in my head was saying, 'this is your moment daughter, be happy, be proud.'

And I realised, with a rush of happiness, that his was indeed my moment. All my life I had lived under another man's name. Now, as each of the Orange men and the members of the memorial band came to shake my hand they were acknowledging me as my father's daughter. This was my moment of recognition, of acceptance. I was Sergeant Bertie White's daughter. They continued to come. All to shake my hand, to pay their respects. So, I smiled most charmingly, and behaved most graciously, as befit the Sergeant's daughter. And I was very proud.

SUSAN WITH FLORRIE MEENAGH - THE GIRL BERTIE LEFT BEHIND

CHAPTER THIRTY ONE

Thursday came and I had still to find my grandparents' grave. Grandfather Abraham had been much on my mind over the last few days. A friend of mine, Robert Frizelle, who had written to me in reply to my letter in the local newspaper, said that he remembered him well. Bob, as he asked me to call him, had told me in his letters of meeting my father on his last leave home before Arnhem. Derek and I went to tea with him and his wife one afternoon at their home in Dungannon. As well as giving me a good description of my father Bob remembered grandfather Abraham. He said how, years after the war, he had often seen the old man waiting at the roadside for his boy to come home.

I felt an overwhelming sense of sadness for my grandfather, particularly as I had been 15 years of age when he died. If things had worked out differently, if my parents had married, or even if I had been acknowledged as Bertie's daughter, I might have been with him during those last years of his life.

Daisy had made some enquiries among the older members of the family as to the exact location of my grandparents' grave. It seemed Uncle Billy, who lived in Moy, would probably know. We arranged to call in and see him that evening. After tea he would walk with us to the churchyard. In the meantime Doreen and Daisy were to take us on a lightening visit to Belfast.

I was sitting in the back of the car idly looking out of the window when the date, 17th July, came into my head. I couldn't think why it would seem important but for some reason I could not get the date out of my mind. Today was Thursday 13th July, so 17th July, would be next Monday. I suddenly remembered David and Heather shared a birthday in July.

"I must remember to buy something for David and Heather's birthday next week," I said out loud.

"What day is their birthday?" asked Doreen.

"Monday, 17th July," I replied, but even as I said it I realised I was wrong. The funny thing was I couldn't recall the date of my son's birthday, only that it was sometime in July. I went through each day in July in my mind hoping this would job my memory. I was completely stuck on 17th July. I realised I was experiencing a mind block.

Having a strong psychic sense means that from time to time I go into what I can only describe as a kind of mind lock. Some information such as a name, a place, a date, or, something that will prove to be of particular significance in the near future, comes into the forefront of my mind. When this happens it is impossible to push it out of my brain until I discover what relevance it has. I knew, from past experience, all I had to do was wait.

It was later that afternoon, when we were back at the farm house, that the significance became clear. Doreen was sorting out a chart showing the family tree when she came on something interesting.

"Guess what?" she said to me. "I have just come upon another of those strange coincidences you are always telling me."

"What this time? I asked intrigued.

"I was looking up your Grandfather Abraham on our family tree and it seems he shares a birthday with David and Heather, he was born on 17th July 1885."

"That's odd," I agreed.

At that time I didn't feel that I knew Doreen well enough to confide in her about my psychic experiences. Some people are completely unnerved by these experiences and, until I know a person well, I find it wiser to keep such occurrences to myself.

I wasn't sure why my grandfather wanted to contact me but at least I knew the significance of the 17th July. As soon as Doreen uttered the words the block in my mind dissolved. I remembered

David's was born on the 24th July not the 17th.

Uncle Billy lived in one of the houses on the hill that runs into Moy. When he opened the door he shook our hands warmly and said that we he and his wife had been looking forward to meet us. He was still a fine looking man, even though he was now in his 70's and walked with the aid of crutches since he was injured by an IRA bomb.

"We expected you ages ago," he said urgently once we had introduced ourselves. "We need to get up to the churchyard before it gets darks."

The church was at the top of the hill and on the way up he pointed out a chemist shop on the corner of the road.

"That is the spot where the house once stood, where your grandfather and the children used to live before the fire," Uncle Billy informed us.

The chemist shop was a single storey building that took up a sizable plot. I gazed at the chemist shop. "The house was completely burnt out then?"

"It must have been a large house?"

"Three storey, like that one," he pointed to an imposing Georgian style house on the opposite side of the road." It had those large rooms with high ceiling, once the fire caught hold it swept through the place. The children, who were sleeping upstairs, didn't have a chance."

"Aunt Meme says it was started deliberately?"

"It was. No doubt about that," he paused for breath, "and we all knew who started it." He looked at me knowingly. "There was a man who had a grudge against your grandfather. He was seen hanging around this corner late at night just days before the fire. On the night of the fire someone saw him with a candle in hand, standing outside the house."

"They never caught him?"

"Not him, he disappeared that night and never dared show his face in Moy ever again."

We crossed the road and came in sight of the church and the vicarage.

"Now I'm not exactly sure where your grandparents are buried," he said as we entered the churchyard. "I remember your grandfather being buried, over there, up against the fence, but there is nothing to mark the place."

We walked along the boundary fence where he thought the grave might be but there were three unmarked plots and he wasn't sure where grandfather lay.

He shook his head, "It was all so long ago."

He walked up and down again. "That's the best I can do I'm afraid, it was all so long ago."

In normal circumstances I might have settled for that. After all there were three unmarked graves, all within close proximity of each other and so I had a rough idea were my grandfather was buried. But my psychic senses told me grandfather Abraham expected better than that.

"Do you know if my grandmother and the children were buried in the same grave," I asked. We were unable to find their graves when we were here last Sunday."

Uncle Billy look perplexed. "Now that's something else I can't be sure of but it may well be so."

I felt rather frustrated. There must be someway of finding out I thought, records or plans of the churchyard. If only I had more time but tomorrow was Friday our last day. Suddenly I remembered the vicarage.

"Why don't we knock and ask at the vicarage," I suggested, "surely the vicar will know where the records are kept?"

Uncle Billy looked worried, "you won't get much help there," he said.

"But why not?"

He shook his head in a noncommittal way.

"Well I'm going to give it a try," I said crossly. "I've only got one more day so I haven't any time to lose." I marched over to the house with Derek and Uncle Billy following in my wake. The vicarage door was slightly open and I pushed confidently on the bell. No answer. I tried again hanging on the bell a little longer. From inside the house I could hear sound of movement and eventually a middle aged woman opened the door. She looked at me blankly.

"I'm sorry to trouble you this late in the evening," I began pleasantly, "but is it possible for me to have a word with the vicar?"

She looked at me more closely and then looked beyond me to Uncle Billy.

"No sorry," she said shortly, "the vicar's not here at present." She went to shut the door.

I pushed myself forward.

"Look, I'm sorry if I'm a nuisance but I am here on holiday and I haven't much time. My grandparents are buried in the churchyard in an unmarked grave and I would very much like to place some flowers of their grave. Is there anyone you know who might have records or, a plan of the cemetery?"

"She looked at me doubtfully. Well as far as I know there are no plans of the graveyard."

"Is there anyone else who might know?"

"No, there's no one."

I felt as if she wanted to be rid of me and she went to close the door again.

I sighed, what to do now.

"What if I call again in the morning," I said patiently. "Maybe there will be someone here then who could help me?"

"She paused for a moment "No! Don't do that," she said, "I'll give you my telephone number and you can ring me about 9am."

I had to be satisfied with that. So I took down the telephone number and finally she closed the door.

I turned to Uncle Billy who was still waiting, "she says the vicar is not at home."

He shrugged, leaving me to draw my own conclusions.

"Come back to the house and have some supper," he said kindly.

Back at the house a supper or sandwiches, cakes and trifle with cream awaited us. I thought it best to steer the conversation away from my grandparents' grave and so asked Uncle Billy how he remembered my father.

"He was a fine man," he assured me pausing from his supper. "Very keen on the marching band and he was also in the Orange Order, always went to meetings when he was home on leave."

"I saw the memorial plaque in the Orange Hall in Bush."

"Yes," he said thoughtfully, "we both went to the Orange Hall in Bush. I remember that last time Bertie was home on leave, I used to keep his 'collar' for him. Like those you see the men wearing in the parade," he explained."

"Oh, yes I know what you mean," I said.

"Well, that last leave he said to me "Billy if I don't come back I want you to have my collar. Funny, that was the only time he said that to me." He paused for a moment lost in his memories.

"So you kept the collar after Bertie died at Arnhem?" I prompted.

"Yes, and very proud I was to have it. Money was hard to come by in those days and there were many who had to march without collars."

"Do you still have it?"

"No, that's what I was going to tell you," he sounded angry now, "I was asked to lend Bertie's collar to someone who hadn't one of their own. So I did, and he, like a fool, left it in a pub and someone walked off with it so I never saw it again."

"That was a pity."

"Someone took it," he was obviously still angry at the thought of it. "But I walked out of that Orange Hall in Bush never went back and haven't set foot in the place since."

I could see that Uncle Billy was a man of uncompromising principles and I admired him for it.

It was getting late so we said goodbye and drove home to the farm house. I had an uneasy night worrying about Grandfather Abraham. I was anxious about what he would want me to do.

At exactly 9am I telephoned the number the vicar's wife had given me.

"Hello," I said when she answered my call, "I'm the lady who called in at the vicarage last night. I was anxious to find my grandparents' grave in the churchyard."

"Yes, I remember," she replied, "but I'm sorry the plan of the churchyard has been lost and there is nothing I can do to help you."

"But surely there must be some record of the graves," I persisted.

"No I'm sorry I can't help you. Now I shall have to go."

I heard the click of the receiver on the other end of the line. I stood there for a time just holder the receiver. There was nothing more I could go. Or, was there?

***

I was out in the garden, picking sweet peas, when Derek came to find me.

"Well did you get any joy out of the vicar's wife?"

"No, she said she was unable to help me."

"So, what do you want to do now?"

"I'm taking these flowers to put on my grandfather's grave."

"You don't know where it is?"

"It suddenly came to me," I explained, "I don't need to know where my grandfather's grave is because grandfather Abraham knows exactly where his mortal remains are buried. I shall ask him to direct me to the right spot. My psychic sense has not failed me yet, it led me to my father's grave, it led me home to Derrywinner. Surely I can find the right grave now."

"Well, if that's what you want to do lets get going because we have a lot to do on our last day."

I stood in the spot where Uncle Billy had taken us the previous evening. It's up to you now Grandfather, I thought. Then, without thinking, I walked over to the nearest grave and knelling down I place the vase of pink, sweet peas, among the rough mown grass on the unmarked grave.

"This is the best I can to do today Grandfather," I said silently, "but I promise you that I shall not forget any of you. You are my family and when I go home I will write a book about my search for Bertie to put the record straight."

A feeling of deep sadness remained with me for some time after we left Moy church. I recalled how grandfather Abraham had waiting for his beloved son to come home. Bertie never came home but I had come in his place. I hope this in some way has put grandfather Abraham's spirit to rest.

CHAPTER THIRTY TWO

There was much to do when we left Moy church. It was our last day and I wanted to do some last minute shopping in Dungannon. The town was crowded after the two days holiday and I was stopped by several people we had met during the previous days.

"I'm beginning to feel more at home here than in Norwich," I said to Derek.

"In some ways this is your home."

And it was true. Generations of my family had lived, and were still living, in this area. All my life I had felt like a misplaced person, missing that sense of belonging, and here at last I had found my roots. Coming to Dungannon I realised how much I had missed when Bertie had died at Arnhem. In losing him I had lost my sense of identity.

We did not stay long in Dungannon. I had intended to go back to the farmhouse to start my packing but Daisy had other ideas. There was someone else she wanted me to meet.

"Only if you feel like it Susan," she assured me, "but Richie Dilworth did say he would like to meet you if you had time. We could drive over in the car."

"Weren't the Dilworths related to my father on his mother's side?"

"That's right, Richie is your father's first cousin. But don't feel you have to go," she added quickly, "Richie is a bit deaf nowadays and his memory is not so good, so don't expect too much."

I thought fleetingly of my packing. I had met so many people already perhaps Richie could wait until next time. But something in the back of my mind was telling me to go.

"I'd like to meet Richie," I said firmly, "as long as it's not too much trouble for you. Daisy had given up a lot of her time to drive us round during our stay. I was reluctant to impose on her once again.

"It's no bother to me," she assured me kindly, "if you want to go then let's be off with us."

Derek and I crammed ourselves into the back of Daisy's car for the drive to Moygashel where Richard Dilworth lived. Moygashel is a small town famous for its printed fabrics. I noticed the fabric mills as we drove through the town into a modest housing estate. The houses looked well cared for with neat front gardens.

"I'm not exactly sure where Richie lives,"" Daisy confessed, "but we can always stop and ask."

I noticed a group of young people talking to a boy on a motor bike. Daisy brought the car to a halt and leaned out of the window.

"Does Richie Dilworth live round here?"

They looked at us, only half interested, and then the boy on the bike said, "right there."

Daisy had stopped the car directly outside Richard Dilworth's house.

Derek and I followed Daisy up the path and stood to one side as she rang the doorbell. The door was opened by an elderly man. He looked at us all in a puzzled way, trying to remember who we were.

"Hello Richie, I've brought Susan, Bertie's daughter, to see you," said Daisy helping him out.

He turned his attention to me, and then he smiled.

"Come on in luv," he said.

Then I remembered that I had lived this moment once before.

I stepped over the doorstep and he held out his hand to me. I looked up into his face and noticed that his eyes were cornflower blue, Then, by some quirk of my grandmother's genes I saw a face that was strikingly like my own. In fact Richie Dilworth could easily have passed as my father.

He showed us into a pleasant living room, where I couldn't help but notice the large bookcase crammed with books, many of titles I had read myself. It seemed Richie and I had more in common than facial similarity. It was a strange meeting. Richie and I sat gazing at each other in awed fascination. I remember being struck by small similarities, the way he smiled, how his two top front teeth crossed in exactly the way mine had before vanity made me have mine capped.

Afterwards, Derek told me, it was at that moment he became absolutely certain I was Bertie White's daughter.

We talked for some time. Richie remembered my grandmother Elizabeth who was a sister of his mother Martha. At times his memory failed him and I could see him struggling to recall those long gone years. He was a quiet, kindly man and I like to think my father would have resembled him. He, good naturedly, allowed me to take some photographs of him. Later I sent him one of these photographs together with one of myself. Seen together the similarity was remarkable.

Richard Dilworth - Bertie's cousin on his mother's side

We returned to the bungalow for our last evening with the family. The Faloons were there in force to say goodbye. With Albert was his brother Trevor, who told me he had always regarded my father as his hero. Sammy Faloon, over from the USA, made up the trio. Albert was on top form with his mad Irish humour and there was much laughter. We were all reluctant to bring the evening to an end but Derek and I had to be up early the next morning for our journey home. And so I bid goodbye to my Faloon cousins.

The night sky was clear and bright, the stars shone brilliantly in the heavens. The moonlight illuminated our way as we walked back to the farmhouse with Doreen and Ken.

"What a wonderful night," said Doreen echoing my thoughts, "let's walk down to the gate."

I remember Doreen telling me that, on the day her sister Arlene had died, she had returned from the hospital deeply distressed. That same night Doreen had walked down to the gate and looked up into the sky above Bertie's field and she felt that Arlene's spirit was out there somewhere and so had been comforted.

We reached the gate and I stood quietly by Doreen's side. The air was warm, the night was silent, eternity stretched above us in the skies.

"They are out there somewhere," I whispered, "Bertie and Arlene and all those who have loved Derrywinner."

On such a night it was easy to imagine the spirits of all those who had lived at Derrywinner joyfully reunited.

CHAPTER THIRTY THREE

I was awake early next morning and I washed and dressed quickly, careful not to disturb the others, then quietly descending the stair, I made my way across the kitchen and let myself out of the back door. I intended to take one last look before it was time to leave.

All was silent and a heavy mist hung in the air giving the barns across the yard a ghostly feel. At the end of the path the empty house by the road loomed mysteriously out of the mist. I stopped for a moment by the gate where we had seen Sandy on our first visit. The family were all so familiar to me now it seemed incredible that just two months ago we were strangers.

The old house was peaceful now, summer roses grew in graceful abundance about the fallen 'For Sale', notice. A pair of house martins had made their nest beneath the broken tiles of the roof. I watched the parent birds darting back and forth, ceaselessly feeding their ravenous brood. How long before some human occupants made the house a home once more?

Passing the barn I noticed the cows and their calves were grazing in Bertie's field. I lifted the handle of the metal barred gate and it squeaked loudly as I pushed it open and passed through. The long grass was wet with drew, soaking through my shoes and the hem of my skirt. Striding out, I made for the far side of the field, just visible now in the morning light. Above me a sky lark sung, rising higher, higher, greeting the first rays of the sun.

I closed my eyes, calling all my senses to remember the moment.

I recalled how, as a child in an alien land, I had tried to make the flowers grow. How, all my life I sought to match the template in my mind of fields and trees and flowers, that had their origin right her at Derrywinner. Radiantly, I lifted my eyes to the rising sun knowing that, at last, my spirit had found its home.

The mist was lifting now, the morning would fulfil its promise of a glorious day. An hour from now and I must leave this place, returning to my own, every day world. Yet, I could not be sad. However far I travelled this was my spiritual home. Here, with Bertie and Arlene and all those who had once loved this place, my spirit would return whenever it had need.

So, turning, I retraced my steps back to the big house, taking with me the joy of the morning, my father Bertie had promised me all those months ago.

CONCLUSION

During September 1995, Derek and I returned to Arnhem for the annual pilgrimage. This time we travelled with a group of Arnhem veterans and next of kin of those who had died. Each year hundreds of such people return for a service of commemoration of the battle of Arnhem held in the war cemetery in Oosterbeek.

If it is possible to say that any good came out of the carnage of 1944, it is the friendship forged between the veterans and the Dutch people. Each September the 'Least we Forget Society' arranges for local volunteers to open their homes and their heart to the pilgrims.

So, it was through them that Derek and I found ourselves the guests of Greet and Haye Drost, in their home in the leafy village of Wolfheze. They not only offered us the sanctuary of their home but a generosity and compassion that one rarely encounters in this modern world. We stayed with Greet and Haye for many Septembers.

With the help of the Arnhem veterans and my friends and family in Ireland, I have slowly piece by piece, built up a picture of the events that shaped my father's life and death. All who remember him tell me of his kindness and his courage. That he was a fine man and a gallant soldier there is no doubt. However, it is not as the Arnhem hero that I like to think of him, but rather, as Florrie Meenagh wrote of him in one of her letters, 'a nice person, quiet in his own way, who smiled often, but always a hint of sadness behind the smile'.

And so, as I come to the end of my story, I look up from my writing and see my father's photograph before me and it is as if his very presence fills the room. Yet, in my heart I feel an awful loneliness, as I know I shall never meet him during this life time. And all my memories of him are second hand.

THE END

IN MEMORY OF
SERGEANT ROBERT GRAHAM (BERTIE) WHITE
WHO DIED AT ARNHEM 18 SEPTEMBER 1944

Printed in Great Britain
by Amazon